D0439319

Canon City Public Library
Canon City, Colorado

Women of The Sierra

Canon City Public Library
Canon City, Colorado

WOMEN OF THE SIERRA
by Anne Seagraves ©1990
Revised Printing: 1992

Other non-fiction books by Anne Seagraves:

Daughters of the West: ©1996

Soiled Doves: Prostitution in the Early West: ©1994

High Spirited Women of the West: ©1992

Women Who Charmed the West: ©1991

Tahoe Lake in the Sky: ©1987

Beautiful Lake County: ©1985

$20.00
SEAGRAVES

Women of The Sierra

By Anne Seagraves

Copyright © 1990 by WESANNE Publications
Printed in the United States of America

Published by WESANNE Publications
Post Office Box 428
Hayden, Idaho 83835

Library of Congress Number 90-70264
ISBN 0-9619088-1-5

ACKNOWLEDGMENTS

Carson Valley Historical Society; Douglas County Library; El Dorado County Chamber of Commerce; El Dorado County Historical Museum; Georgetown Library; Lake County Library, Lakeport; Lake County Museum; Lake Tahoe Historical Society; Nevada County Library; Nevada Historical Society; Nevada State Library; North Lake Tahoe Historical Society; Pajaro Valley Historical Association; Searls Historical Library; Washoe County Parks and Recreation, Bowers' Mansion; Watsonville Public Library.

While researching Women of the Sierra many individuals and organizations have been extremely helpful. The author would like to express her appreciation to these people and organizations.

Luetta Dressler Bergevin, for sharing her information and photographs of Eliza Cook, M.D.; Miriam Biro and Lillian Wyman, North Lake Tahoe Historical Society, for the Ethel Joslin Vernon story; Evelyn E. Lyon Meyers, for Sierra Nevada Phillips; Beatrice Fettic Jones, for sharing her information and photographs of Eliza Mott; Lillian Bergevin, for Agnes Thompson, a story that was deleted due to insufficient historical data; Shirley Taylor, for sharing personal stories and photographs of Amelia Celio; For the Lillie Langtry story: Orville Magoon, Proprietor of Guenoc Winery, for releasing photographs from his private collection, Donna Howard, Curator of the Lake County Museum and Marion Goeble, Lake County Historian, for their valuable historical data and photographs; F.N. Fossati and his wife Irene, and Joe Cola, for stories and photographs of Sara Fossati; Searls Historical Library for their time and effort in locating information about Lotta Crabtree, Lola Montez, and Juanita; The Pajaro Valley Historical Association and the Watsonville Public Library for contributing to the story of Charlotte "Charley" Parkhurst; The Georgetown Library, El Dorado County Chamber of Commerce, The El Dorado County Historical Museum, and the book Maude Hulbert Horn by Nora Beale Jacobs, for the story of Maude Hulbert Horn. And Beverly Cola, Curator, El Dorado County Historical Museum for digging up old photos and information about Sierra Nevada Phillips; Amelia Celio; Maude Hulbert Horn; Charlotte "Charley" Parkhurst, and Sarah Fossati, and, for always having the right answer to historic questions.

And a Very Special Thank You to:

Louise Talley, for her constant support and encouragement throughout the writing of this book. And to the editors: Wes Seagraves, Louise Talley, and David Stoneberg.

The Sierra Nevada Range is a mountainous chain extending along the eastern border of the state, more than 400 miles long and about 70 miles wide. Its terrain rises gently from the central valley of California to an abrupt series of inclines leading into the plains of Nevada. The entire range is known for its scenic beauty, vast wilderness, and inhospitable winter weather.

Between the 1840s and 1880s, the Northern Sierra experienced a rapid growth. Gold was discovered in 1848 at Sutter's Mill, and by 1849 thousands of prospectors started arriving. Prices for food and lodging went sky-high as the eager miners rushed in to stake their claims throughout what is known today as the Mother Lode. Shacks rented for as much as $100 a week, and the price was $15 for a night on a cot. Due to the mass emigration of the 1850s, the territory of California had enough people to qualify as a state.

In 1859 one of the richest silver finds was discovered in the Comstock, and adventurers flocked to the diggings. Virginia City grew from a handful of people to a large mining center where miners lived in tents, stone huts, or a hole in the hillside. Supplies had to be hauled over the mountains from California.

Both the Mother Lode and the Comstock were filled with men who came from all over the nation to seek their fortunes in the gold fields and later in the silver mines. Due to the lack of housing and the expensive cost of living, most of the women and children remained behind. It became a man's world filled with gun-toting rowdies and prospectors who worked hard and drank heavily and, in most cases, did not find either the gold or silver they were seeking.

Since there were few women in the Sierra, prostitution and gambling became an important part of the lonely miners' lives. The arrival of their wives and children brought a measure of morality and comfort into the area and put an end to most of the red-light districts. Many of the "ladies" moved on to newer territory. The area itself, however, remained an untamed, lawless place until the latter part of the century when the mining camps grew into respectable communities.

Dedicated to the Women...
Who met the demands of Yesterday...
Fulfilled the promises of Today...
And are ready for the challenges of Tomorrow.

CONTENTS

Cover Photo: Eliza Cook, M.D.
Courtesy of Luetta Dressler Bergevin

This is a collection of stories about women achievers of the mid-1800s through the turn-of-the-century. They are the gallant ladies who helped to shape the colorful history of the Sierra. Each one is unique...all made a valuable contribution to the area.

When writing about the Sierra, it is difficult to separate fact from fiction. There are many legends, and tall-tales, mixed in with the true stories of the pioneers who settled the inhospitable land. First there were the prospectors who came in search of gold or silver. It was a man's world with few amenities, and remained that way until the latter part of the 19th century.

By the early 1850s, women were beginning to arrive in the Sierra. Most of them traveled across the plains or over the dangerous Isthmus of Panama. Some took the perilous journey by sea around Cape Horn. Although the women's companionship and their ability to work was appreciated by the men, very little was written about them. No doubt there are many women who deserve to be recognized in this publication, and the author sincerely regrets that their stories can't be told.

The first women to appear were prostitutes like Julia Bulette, the "Queen of the Red-Light District." Her brutal murder made Julia a legend in Virginia City. Eilley Orrum, another early arrival, was a hard-working woman who fought her way from poverty in the Highlands of Scotland to wealth in the Comstock only to lose it all in the end. There were actresses like the famous Lillie Langtry, America's first superstar; Grass Valley's notorious Lola Montez with her fiery temper and sensual "Spider Dance;" and the loveable Lotta Crabtree, a "Fairy Star" who romped her way into the hearts of the miners and became America's first comedienne.

Into the Mormon territory came Eliza Cook, M.D., Nevada's first woman doctor. She dared to walk the path of prejudice and entered a male-dominated profession. Eliza Mott, a dedicated wife and mother from Mottsville, became Nevada's first teacher and opened a school in her kitchen.

In Downieville the tragic Juanita was denied the right of a fair trial and was hung by a frenzied mob. Nevada City was the site of Eleanora Dumont's first gambling saloon. Later Eleanora became known as

"Madame Moustache." Traveling the mountainous trails was Charlotte "Charley" Parkhurst, a disillusioned woman who posed as a man and drove stage with such noted Jehu (Knights of the Lash) as Hank Monk.

In Georgetown Maude Hulbert Horn became a 19th-century publisher and later Justice of the Peace. The Placerville area had Sarah Fossati who was an astute businesswoman long before her time. The Tahoe region was enhanced by Ethel Joslin Vernon, Poetess of the Sierra, and Amelia Celio, a gentle woman who helped in the annual cattle drives and made all of her own furniture. And there was the energetic Sierra Nevada Phillips, a woman called "Vade" who was known throughout the Sierra for her fine resorts.

In this book the author has presented a diverse variety of women and shown the importance of their roles in the 19th-century. They were the free-spirited women of the Sierra. From doctor to innkeeper, these female pioneers achieved their independence in a male-dominated society and opened the doors for others to follow.

---◆---

In order to write this book,
thousands of pages have been researched, along with
numerous newspaper columns and personal interviews.
In some instances, there were conflicting records or statements,
and many times a story was incomplete.
In this book I have attempted to provide an accurate account
of these noteworthy women and their lives.
— The Author

◆———————————◆

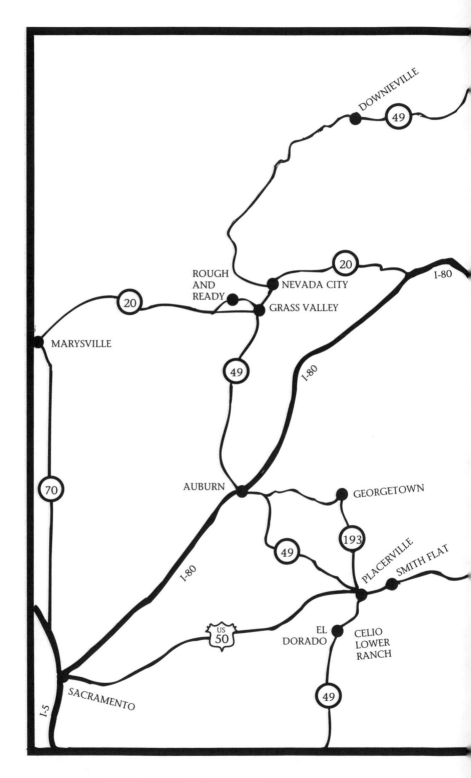

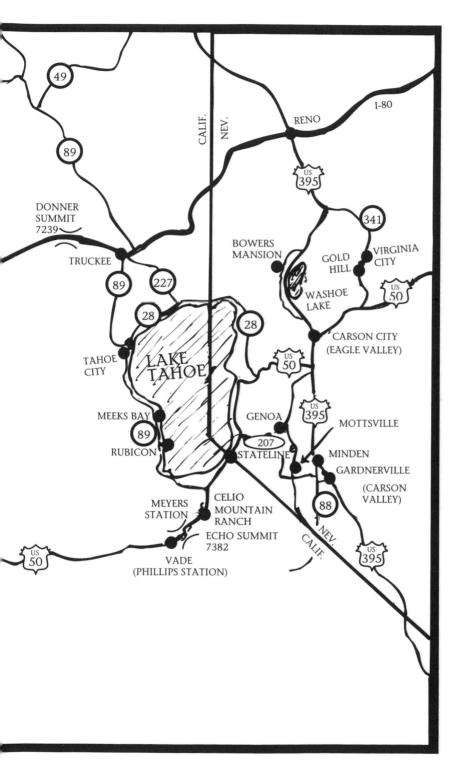

Courtesy of Luetta Dressler Bergevin

◆─────────────────────────◆

Eliza Cook, M.D. In 1884, at the age of 28, Eliza Cook became Nevada's first woman doctor. She successfully practiced medicine in the Carson Valley for over 40 years.

Chapter 1

ELIZA COOK

Nevada's First Woman Doctor

In the 1890s Dr. M. Cary Thomas requested permission to attend a class at Johns Hopkins University School of Medicine in Baltimore, Maryland. She dared to tread where no other woman had been allowed. She was accepted only on the condition that she sit behind a screen. Later, Dr. Thomas became president of Bryn Mawr College.

Dr. Eliza Cook also dared to walk the path of prejudice to enter a "man's field." Eliza became Nevada's first woman doctor in 1884, and she successfully practiced medicine in the Carson Valley for over 40 years.

Eliza cook was born on February 5, 1856, in Salt Lake City and moved to the Carson Valley with her mother and sister in 1870. They lived with Eliza's uncle who had settled near Sheridan.

When her mother died, Eliza, who had always been interested in medicine, became a nurse to Dr. H. H. Smith of Genoa. He was so impressed with the young woman's skill and ability in the care of the ill that he encouraged her to study medicine. Eliza became his assistant as well as his student, and, with the doctor's help, she was accepted at the Cooper School of Medicine in San Francisco. The college later became part of Stanford University.

In 1884, at the age of 28, Eliza received her medical degree. She had completed the customary two years of study required at that time and returned home to practice.

Doctors were scarce in the 1800s, especially in the large sprawling Carson Valley where freezing winter storms frequently pounded the Sierra. The erect figure of Dr. Cook, and her black buggy, soon became a welcome sight throughout the area. No matter how late the hour or how far she had to travel, the dedicated doctor answered the call to attend the needs of the ill and injured. She traveled icy roads, fought blizzards, and crossed flooded rivers to complete her rounds and care for her patients. Late at night, returning home cold and weary, Eliza could always tell the time by the lights shining in the windows of the various ranches in the valley. She had traveled the area so many times that she knew the habits of each family.

On many occasions, Dr. Cook was summoned by a frantic husband to deliver a baby. When she had completed her professional duties, Eliza would return each day for two weeks to bathe the child (she loved babies) and care for the mother. In many instances, Eliza would also help the family by cooking and cleaning until the mother could assume the household chores.

Eliza was a tall, slender woman with dark hair pulled severely back from her intelligent, pretty face. She wore long black coats and dresses with high-stemmed collars adorned by a simple brooch. She called her patients by their first names and was considered a lady who "went along with the times." Eliza often frowned on girls wearing socks instead of stockings, but would shrug her shoulders and say "things change." She was always proper, and when dancing, she was careful to keep a "safe distance" from her partner.

Although Eliza often appeared severe and professional, she was a warm, kind, dedicated person. She was loved by all and affectionately called "Auntie" by her devoted nieces and nephews, as well as the other local children. Many times a sick child would be frightened at the sight of Eliza's dark apparel and black buggy. In order to dispel this fear, Eliza would bake cookies and take them to the children she treated.

Dr. Cook never married; however, she was considered a wonderful homemaker. Her seven-room house, near Mottsville, was set against the backdrop of the Sierra. The large kitchen was the focal point for entertainment. There she cooked fine food on a tiny three-foot woodstove with an oven that opened on both sides. Dr. Cook had a special cup without handles that she would hold to warm her hands after a cold day of caring for the ill.

Eliza had a deep love of nature and growing things. Her home was surrounded by lovely flowers, and behind it there was a large apple orchard that she irrigated and cared for herself. In the autumn the scent of apples stored in her cool pantry filled the air. She made delicious applesauce, apple butter, and preserves that were delivered to her patients and friends. Eliza also crocheted, tatted, and made exquisite lace creations that are carefully wrapped and lovingly kept at the home of her great-grand niece in Gardnerville.

As well as an expert physician, she was also a pharmacist. Dr. Cook set broken limbs with splints she made herself and skillfully prepared prescriptions on a little apothecary scale. It was kept on a table in her dining room where she measured the exact dose of medicinal powders. She would wrap the medication in a small piece of white tissue approximately 4 inches by 5 inches and fold it to an oblong size encasing the powders. Each dose was numbered, then placed in an envelope with the patient's name, date, and instructions for dispensing. Members of her family saved tissue paper for her home-operated pharmacy. Each piece was carefully sterilized with dry heat and cut to the required size.

Eliza was extremely well-read and traveled extensively during her lifetime. She gave frequent lectures and was a respected speaker as well as dedicated doctor. Although Eliza was disciplined and stern in her profession, she was always sympathetic with young people. She would spend hours helping them find out who they were and stressed the importance of doing what they enjoyed. Her many deeds inspired others to become involved in medicine.

In 1894 Eliza Cook became an ardent member of the woman's suffrage movement. In addition to her already heavy schedule, she managed to actively support women's rights, finding the time to lecture and to circulate petitions. Dr. Cook strongly believed there were many injustices in the social system and worked hard to help overcome them.

Eliza practiced medicine for over 40 years in the Carson Valley. In her last years of caring for patients, Eliza put her horse and buggy away and started driving a Model T. She retired in the late 1920s, and many of the babies she delivered during her career still live in the valley.

Death for Dr. Eliza Cook was met with her usual acceptance of life. She passed away quietly, in 1947, at age 91, at home in her own bed. She must have had a premonition that her time was near. Her home was in order and her hands were peacefully folded upon her breast. Eliza's life had been fulfilled.

DR. ELIZA COOK'S
REASONS FOR HER INVOLVEMENT
IN THE WOMEN'S MOVEMENT

1. Because I am a native American and citizen of the United States, but do not feel like one unless I have the rights and privileges of the masculine citizen.

2. Because taxation without representation is tyranny in the case of women, as well as men.

3. Because no citizen can represent another at the polls. If he can, why not vote by proxy?

4. Because being a woman, I can see things from a woman's viewpoint. Hence, no man, however willing he might be to suppress his own view in my behalf, could represent me fully at the ballot box or anywhere else.

5. Because man cannot fill woman's place in the economy of nature, nor in socio-economy. How then can he fill her place in the political economy of the nation?

6. Because I believe in the fullest development of every human being. I believe the responsibility of citizenship will arouse the dormant powers of our women.

7. Because I believe women fully as capable of assisting in the government of the home. Though I have heard until I am tired that woman cannot fight, and therefore should not vote, I still believe that when men are on the battlefield they cannot be at home, and consequently, women have to do their work and that of the man.

8. Because I, an adult American woman, am opposed to being placed politically on par with the convict, the insane, the idiot, the Indian and the minor, and below the ignorant foreigner who cannot read or write his own name.

9. Because if the right to vote is the evidence of a man's freedom and citizenship, the absence of that right shows that woman is neither free nor a citizen.

10.Because I believe in justice to all, and feel that there is no justice in denying the ballot to one-half of humanity because of a difference of physical confirmation, since there can be no doubt that man, with the same mentality as woman would be allowed to vote as the lowest specimen of the masculine gender, rather the exceptions noted are allowed a voice in the affairs of our government.

11. Because I believe in the natural equality of the sexes before the laws, political, social and moral, etc.

Genoa Weekly-Courier, December 1894

As a result of Dr. Cook's efforts, and those of many other suffragettes, the Nineteenth Amendment became a part of the Constitution of the United States in August, 1920, and all women received full voting privileges.

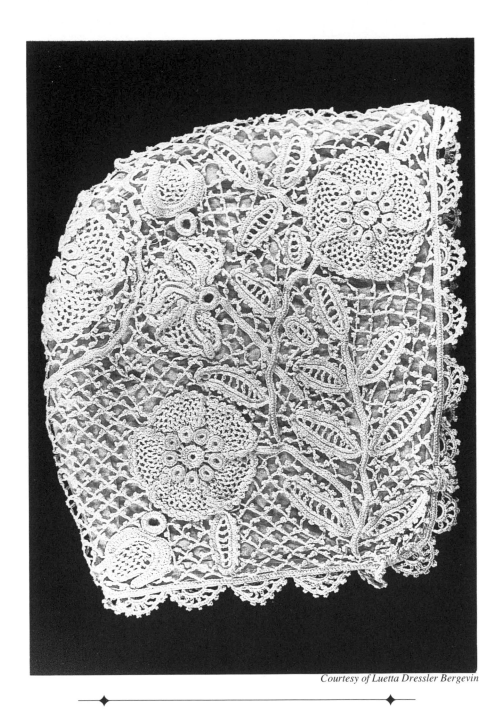

Courtesy of Luetta Dressler Bergevin

*Baby cap crocheted in 1921 by Eliza Cook, M.D.
for Luetta Dressler Bergevin. Luetta is Eliza's great-grand niece,
and she was the last baby delivered by Dr. Cook.*

The residence of Eliza Cook, M.D.
Dr. Cook is standing in the door.

Courtesy of The Nevada Historical Society

The seven-room home, near Mottsville,
is set against the backdrop of the Sierra, and is still standing today.

Drawing by Robin Isely

Just Juanita

Chapter 2

JUANITA

First White Woman Lynched in California

O n the fourth of July, 1851, Downieville celebrated the anniversary of the birth of our republic. The tents, cabins, and buildings were decorated with flags, and hundreds of miners were in town for the event. They consumed large amounts of alcohol and presented lively speeches from a large platform in the town square. One after another, the orators proclaimed the right of liberty for all and declared all men were free.

However, something went wrong in Downieville. The next day these same people participated in one of the most shocking crimes in California history...they allowed a frenzied mob to hang a woman without the constitutional right to a fair trial. The speeches about equality and liberty for all obviously were not meant to include women, especially of the Mexican race. The victim was Juanita, and her name will be forever linked with the area's colorful past.

Juanita (no last name was ever recorded) was considered attractive, with long, lustrous dark hair; delicate features; and passionate black eyes. She was a graceful young woman from Sonora, Mexico, who was reputed to have been a saloon girl at one time. In Downieville, however, she was considered a better class woman than the camp followers. She lived with her lover in a small cabin, and, although many men sought her favors, Juanita was content with her man, José.

They were a happy couple. José was a quiet, simple man who dealt cards at Craycroft's Saloon. In contrast, Juanita was noted for her hot-blooded Latin temper and brightly colored skirts. She met José after work every night, and they would walk home together holding hands in the moonlight.

On the day of the crime, July 5, 1851, the Independence Day celebration had continued into the early morning hours when several of the revelers staggered from the saloons. Some were in high spirits, singing and laughing; other's were drunken vandals who went down the streets breaking open the doors of houses. Jack Cannon was one of the latter. He was a large Scotsman who was popular with the men and considered to be a camp rowdy.

On this particular morning, some say Cannon fell against the door of José and Juanita's cabin knocking it from its hinges. It also has been said he offered her a bag of gold, and when she said "no," he kicked his way into her cabin smashing the door. Whatever the true story, Juanita asked Cannon to leave her alone. He called her obscene names in Spanish and accused her of being a prostitute. He also said she was just a Mexican woman who thought she was too good for him. Juanita swore back at Cannon, and he put her door back in place and left.

After a few hours of sleep, Cannon returned to Juanita's cabin. It is not known whether it was to apologize or to seduce her. José came out and politely asked to have his door repaired. Cannon, who was suffering from a hangover, started once more to insult both Juanita and José. The argument became louder, and a crowd began to form. Juanita, upset by the insults and the audience's jeers, asked Cannon to be quiet and invited him into her house to talk. At this point, it is not clear what happened. Either the large man lunged at her, or Juanita's temper became too violent. She grabbed a Bowie knife, and, small and slender though she was, she managed to plunge the knife into Cannon's chest, instantly killing him.

The stunned spectators, realizing their friend was dead, started yelling, "Lynch them!" In fear, Juanita and José ran to Craycroft's where they thought they would find protection. The angry mob surrounded the saloon, and the couple's defenders were forced to run for their own lives. There was no escape for Juanita. She was dragged to the main plaza and forced upon the same platform where the public speeches were heard the day before. Cannon's body, with its ugly wound, was placed nearby to inflame the crowd.

"Hang them!" the mob shouted. "Not without a trial," others responded. A judge and jury were selected along with attorneys for the prosecution and the defense. The scene was set for a mock trial, and the spectators settled down to watch. The young defense attorney called upon friends and relatives to speak for Juanita. He begged those present to remember their loved ones and to spare the young woman, beseeching them not to shed her blood. The mob kicked the barrel from beneath his feet. They threw him into the crowd breaking his glasses. He was kicked and received blows from all sides.

Witnesses called by the prosecutor said they saw the stabbing, but none attempted to find out why. Some said the insults were nothing to be mad about and discussed the "evil temperament" of all Mexican women. Dr. C. D. Aiken declared Juanita was pregnant, and for that reason she should not be hung. Three other doctors examined her and said she was not pregnant. Dr. Aiken was given 24 hours to leave town.

The crowd's mood became uglier as the "trial" continued. The jury found Juanita guilty. She was sentenced to death by hanging within the hour and denied the solace of a priest. They took the trembling 22-year-old woman to a nearby cabin to wait for her death. The mob shouted curses and eagerly awaited the hanging.

Juanita had one hour to prepare. No one will ever know what she thought about during that hour. Did she cry for her lover José who had been forced to leave town? Alone in the cabin, it can be assumed she prayed for forgiveness and the courage to accept her fate.

A rope was hung from the top of the Jersey Bridge. Beneath it a plank swung out over the river. Townspeople lined the streets to see the hanging. The air was hot, and empty whiskey barrels still lay on the ground from the night before.

Juanita was taken from her cabin, and with her head held high, she bravely faced the crowd. She searched the group for a friendly face, and, finding one, smiled sadly and said "Adios, amigo, adios," and threw him her straw hat. Juanita's thick dark hair came cascading down around her slender shoulders. She took the noose in her own hands and placed it around her neck. They tied her arms, skirt, and feet together...within seconds Juanita was dead. Most of the spectators returned to the Downieville saloons.

This infamous miscarriage of justice was heard around the world. *The London Times* condemned the "border justice." Other newspapers said she was a "friendless and unprotected foreigner."

It will never be known if Juanita was innocent or guilty. Although Chinese and Indian women had been hung, Juanita was the first woman who was denied the right of a fair trial. She was buried next to Cannon, and the legend of her hanging lives on.

On September 14, 1986, Naomi Parlor No. 36, Native Daughters of the Golden West, dedicated a monument and plaque in Heritage Park, Downieville, California, to the memory of Juanita, commemorating a colorful chapter in the history of the gold rush community.

"Hanging of a Woman:"

"The occurrence which was published a few days ago, as having taken place at Downieville, proves to be no fiction as several papers supposed. John S. Fowler, Esq., who witnessed the frightful scene, describes the affair as reflecting infinite disgrace upon all engaged in it. The act for which the victim suffered, was one entirely justifiable under the provocation. She stabbed a man who persisted in making a disturbance at her house and had greatly outraged her rights."

"The violent proceedings of an indignant and excited mob led on by the enemies of the unfortunate woman are a blot upon the history of the state. Had she committed a crime of really heinous character, a real American would have revolted at such a course as was pursued toward this friendless and unprotected foreigner. We had hoped the story was fabricated. As it is, the perpetrators of the deed have shamed themselves and their race. The Mexican woman is said to have borne herself with the utmost of fortitude and composure through the fearful ordeal, meeting her fate without flinching."

Daily Alta California, July 14, 1852

Courtesy of The North Lake Tahoe Historical Society

Ethel Joslin Vernon on her honeymoon in October, 1911.

Chapter 3

ETHEL JOSLIN VERNON

✦ Poetess of the Sierra ✦

"Know you the haunts of the clean Sierran Highland...
The crash of foaming water down a mossy granite stair?
Have you trod the dim trails across the twilit skyland,
And watched the sunset flame and die beyond the cloud-land there?
Then you have touched God's footstool on the floor of upper air."
    By Ethel Joslin Vernon
    From her book, Through the Rainbow Gate
    Courtesy of the North Lake Tahoe Historical Society

Although Ethel Joslin Vernon was not a true pioneer, having arrived in Tahoe City in 1909, no one has captured the beauty of the Sierra as well as she did.

Ethel Joslin Vernon was born June 25, 1890, in a log cabin in Pineville, Missouri. At the age of five, she moved with her mother to Perris, a small community in southern California. Her mother died about the time Ethel completed sixth grade, and the young girl was taken in by relatives. Later, she found employment in a laundry where she helped to support herself while continuing her education.

Ethel first read about the spectacular beauty of the Sierra and Lake Tahoe in a school geography class. The description interested her so much that she answered an ad for employment at The Tahoe Tavern. Ethel was hired immediately, and, with a prayer in her heart and borrowed rail fare, she left for Tahoe City.

When she arrived on the North Shore of Lake Tahoe, in June 1909, Ethel was spellbound by the majestic mountains and vast forests that surrounded the deep blue lake. It was a religious experience that filled her with reverence and the knowledge that this was home. She also met William "Bill" Vernon of Lake Elsinor, California, who had already arrived to work as a musician at The Tahoe Tavern during the summer season.

The following year, both Ethel and Bill returned to the tavern where they fell in love and became engaged. They were married in October, 1911, at the Methodist Church in Truckee. The next day the groom had a surprise honeymoon planned. It was a trip around Lake Tahoe in a double-oared rowboat! Most young women would have been upset, but the groom knew of his new bride's insatiable hunger for nature and wanted to help her fulfill it.

The adventurous couple packed equipment and supplies aboard the boat, and, in the unpredictable month of October, started on the memorable trip. They fished, hunted, and explored the scenic shoreline, and slept under a myraid of stars. When the waves became high, they stayed close to shore. The newlyweds purchased groceries at the different communities around the lake, making new friends as they traveled. They rowed out to meet the steamer, Tahoe, to pick up their mail. The trip lasted almost three weeks and intensified Ethel's childhood dreams of communicating her love of nature through poetry and song.

Following the honeymoon, the Vernons established their home in Riverside, California; however, both had fallen under the spell of the Sierra. They continued to return every summer with their two daughters, Florence and Lillian. In the fall of 1923, Mrs. Vernon suggested they stay through the winter and experience the snow. They enjoyed the season so much that Lake Tahoe became their home. In her newfound happiness, Ethel started wearing a fresh red rosebud every day.

Mrs. Vernon had learned, while living in Riverside, that she was a natural poet. There she wrote Indian lore and poetry for the *Los Angeles Times* under the pen name of June Melody. At Tahoe, she signed her name, Ethel Joslin Vernon, and began writing for newspapers like *The Sacramento Bee*, *Auburn Journal*, and *Sierra Sun*, in Truckee. Editors complimented her perfect copies which needed no corrections. She was praised for the use of words that they said must come from the depth of her soul.

Ethel explored the foot trails of the wilderness accompanied by her dog "Sky Boy." Together they traveled to the high places where few had been. They shared the splendor of an indigo-blue lake at their feet, sweeping panoramas, and quiet coves. Ethel reached out and touched the trees and wild creatures of the woods, and they touched her back. She learned the continuance of the future and acceptance of death. She was at peace with herself and, through her poems, both expressed and shared her emotions. Ethel had a unique skill of precision and rhythm with a style of space and line that few poets have shared.

In 1944, Ethel published her first book, *A Voice from the Mountain Top*, her next book was titled *Tahoe Trails and Mountain Memories*. In 1950, Mrs. Vernon was invited to join the Poets of the Pacific, Inc., in San Francisco. She did join, and became a member of the Board of Directors and elected to publish the annual Anthology. Ethel resigned in 1953, and began to publish her own poetry magazine at home on a portable typewriter. In her next book, *Through the Rainbow Gate*, she added illustrations. Ethel was a fine artist, as well as a photographer. Her sketches and pictures were filled with meaning and expression. In her fourth book, *Valley of the Start*, she also offered inspirational illustrations.

On her last hike up a long trail that led to the crest of a mountain, Ethel was so awed by the scene that she wrote the poem, "Aspiration." The poem had such a religious theme that it was made into a hymn and the name changed to "Hymn of the Sierra." This was part of an unfulfilled dream for Mrs. Vernon, who had recorded her lyrics for 55 years, always hoping they would be set to music. She decorated the cover sheet for the hymn with a pen-and-ink drawing of two hands holding folded strains of music.

Ethel also showed her artistry in the weaving of pine needle baskets and mats with designs never done by Indian craftsmen. She used feather stitching, and her many creations were displayed in gift shops. Her symmetrically-perfect work has been taken all over the United States and parts of Europe. Many of her baskets are still on display at the Gatekeeper's Museum in Tahoe City.

In 1964, at age 74, Mrs. Vernon's health began to fail and she gave up all writing. She had sensed the end was near and expressed the hope that she would die in her sleep...her wish was granted. Ethel Joslin Vernon died in her sleep on Christmas Eve. Services were held at the Tahoe Episcopal Church, and it was appropriate that the minister should quote her poem, "A Mountain Poet's Prayer," and that her "Hymn of the Sierra" be played softly on the church organ.

Ethel Joslin Vernon was many things to the Sierra: a poet, photographer, artist, and most of all, a friend. She climbed to great heights and inspired the hearts of many. She was a unique woman who achieved her success through the goodness within herself. A simple plaque dedicated and placed as the headstone on her grave reads: "True poetry is the voice of beauty, and beauty is in the heart of God."

Privileged

◆

Know you the haunts of the clean Sierran highland...
The crash of foaming water down a mossy granite stair?
Have you trod the dim trails across the twilit skyland,
And watched the sunset flame and die beyond the cloud-land there?
Then you have touched God's footstool on the floor of upper air.

Know you the silence of the range-top at dawning...
Have you heard the peaks awake before the stars have dimmed?
Have you stood on dizzy heights to view the chasm yawning,
And watched the ragged skyline with the rosy morning rimmed?
Then you have heard God whisper, and His early masses hymned.

Know you the peace of the night upon the highland...
The mystery of moonlight down the forest aisle?
Have you seen the millions of stars that roof the skyland,
And watched the planets whirling down Infinity's long mile?
Then you have looked into God's face and felt His healing smile.

From the book, Through the Rainbow Gate
By Ethel Joslin Vernon

Courtesy of The North Lake Tahoe Historical Society

◆   ◆

From the book, Through the Rainbow Gate, Courtesy of The North Lake Tahoe Historical Society

Aspiration

What if the world be blind and deaf,
And what care I if the world be dumb?
My soul can see to turn the key,
And the melody from my heart will come.

I'll hold my Song in my hands at last
And stand tip-toe beneath the skies...
And scatter its bars among the stars
To glitter and throb in Heaven's eyes!

From the book, Through the Rainbow Gate
By Ethel Joslin Vernon

Courtesy of The North Lake Tahoe Historical Society

Courtesy of The North Lake Tahoe Historical Society

Ethel Joslin Vernon, Poetess of the Sierra,
June, 1911, the year she became engaged to marry
William "Bill" Vernon.

Courtesy of The North Lake Tahoe Historical Society

◆ ━━━━━━━━━━━━━━━━━━━━━━━━━━━━━━━━ ◆

William "Bill" Vernon,
June, 1911, the year he became engaged to marry
Ethel Joslin.

The Tahoe Tavern
Established 1901 • Demolished 1964

Ethel and Bill met and fell in love at the tavern.

*Ethel Joslin Vernon's symmetrically-perfect baskets
on display at The Gatekeeper's Museum at Tahoe City, California.*

Courtesy of The El Dorado County Historical Museum

◆———————————————————————◆

Sierra Nevada Phillips, an energetic woman called "Vade,"
who did not know the meaning of "impossible" and was known
throughout the Sierra as "Mrs. Hospitality."

♦

Chapter 4

SIERRA NEVADA PHILLIPS
A Woman Called "Vade"

S ierra Nevada Phillips was an energetic woman called "Vade." She was a lady with a warm natural personality who did not know the meaning of the word "impossible." During her lifetime, Vade owned and operated many popular resorts in the Sierra. She was one of the best cooks in the area and had a large clientele who followed her wherever she went.

Vade was the daughter of J. W. Phillips and his wife Mehitable Jane Ball. In 1851, they left their home in Vermont and traveled to the gold fields of California via the Panama route. The couple tried mining and then moved to El Dorado County, where they purchased 160 acres of beautiful meadowland, near the American River. There was a heavy flow of traffic along the "Great Bonanza Road" to the Comstock, and in 1863, they built a two-and-one-half-story resort on their property. It was called Phillips Station and became one of the busiest stations along the dirt thoroughfare.

Mehitable was known for her fine meals, and she taught her daughter Vade, at an early age, how to prepare food. When she was 12, the young girl decided to become the best cook in the Sierra. She overheard one of the teamsters tell her father that, because Mrs. Phillips was away for the evening, he supposed they weren't going to get a good meal. Vade went into the kitchen and provided such a tasty supper that the embarrassed man felt compelled to stuff himself.

Sierra Nevada was married twice, first to A. W. Clark and later to James Bryson.

In 1884, she bought the primitive Rubicon Resort and Springs from the Hunsucker brothers, who were unable to cope with the heavy flow of guests. It was located in a wild, remote area with beautiful views, and a road that was little more than a mountainous trail. All supplies had to be brought in by pack mule from barges on Lake Tahoe. Rebuilding the dilapidated resort was a difficult task. Vade, however, was a determined woman, and within three years she managed to erect a new and comfortable two-and-one-half-story hotel in the wilderness.

The establishment had 16 rooms, with curtains at the windows and an elegant parlor with fine furnishings. Sierra Nevada renamed the resort, Rubicon Mineral Springs Hotel and Resort, and advertised the mineral water which was said to be "better than whiskey." Health seekers flocked in over the hazardous trail, and Vade added cabins and tents. The Rubicon spa was very popular with the wealthy Comstockers, and as the traffic increased, Vade realized the need for a better route to the springs. She went to El Dorado County and persuaded them to build a road to Rubicon.

In 1890, Sierra Nevada sold the Rubicon resort and moved to Meeks Bay where she operated a large hall. She added a dairy and laundry, and tents were put up for her following of campers. Later that same year, she decided to rebuild the old Phillips Station where she grew up. All that was left of the half-century-old establishment was one small building and a barn.

It took a year for Vade to develop Phillips into a full-fledged resort with cabins, general store, cocktail lounge and campground. Phillips flourished and became known from coast to coast. The resort catered to families, and many returned every summer. In fact, some came so often that the cabins were named for various families. Among the notable guests listed in the register are former Secretary of State Frank Jordon and former Defense Secretary Robert McNamara, who was 12 years old at the time.

Running a resort in the late 1800s was a difficult chore, but Vade managed to overcome all obstacles. There was no electricity...refrigeration was done in an icehouse by the river, that everyone hoped would hold through the summer. Fruits, vegetables and meats had to be brought in by wagon. Fresh eggs, butter and lard were sent around the lake by steamer, and picked up at Camp Richardson (which was then called the "Grove"). Once the steamer dropped the perishable food off, it had to be picked up immediately. Vade and her daughters, Alice and Mehitable, would go down with a horse and wagon early in the morning, and return late at night.

Later they had daily stage service, and in 1921, the first mechanical equipment appeared over Echo (Highway 50). It was a Nash four-wheeler that was used as a grader by pulling a 12-foot timber with an iron blade. This was quite an improvement over the previous maintenance crew, which consisted of five men with picks and shovels.

Vade had also been a postmistress all of her life. Wherever she went she opened a post office. When Phillips reopened, she went to the postmaster in Placerville requesting a post office for the old station. The name Phillips was taken by another location, so he told her to just call it "Vade."

Sierra Nevada Phillips died at 67, in 1921. She was one of the most dynamic women the Sierra had known. During her active lifetime, she went through the horse and buggy era into the mechanical age of today. And, although Phillips Station has been gone for years, a woman called Vade, who was respected throughout the Sierra, as "Mrs. Hospitality," is fondly remembered.

Courtesy of The El Dorado County Historical Museum

"Vade" on her horse "Beck."

Courtesy of The El Dorado County Historical Museum

◆━━━━━━━━━━━━━━━━━◆

*Family photo taken in 1903. On the left, Mehitable Jane Clark Sickles
(Vade's daughter from her first marriage) holding Wells Sickles,
Vade's grandson, Vade (center) holding her daughter Alice
(Vade's daughter from her second marriage) and
Mehitable Jane Ball Phillips, Vade's mother.*

RUBICON MINERAL SPRINGS HOTEL
established in 1886 by Mrs. Vade Clark.

From the book, I Remember, Courtesy of The El Dorado County Chamber of Commerce

◆――――――――――――――――――――――◆

Vade operated the 16-room hotel for 15 years,
marketing the water she said was "better than whiskey."

Courtesy of Beatrice Fettic Jones

Eliza Ann Middaugh Mott, Nevada's first teacher.

Chapter 5

ELIZA MOTT

Nevada's First Schoolteacher

In 1854 Eliza Mott recognized the need for education in the Carson Valley, and she decided to do something about it. The dedicated wife and mother started the first school in Nevada in her own home and became the state's first schoolteacher.

Due to her achievements in the field of learning, education became important in that area. Two years later the first official organization of school districts was established.

Eliza Ann Middaugh was born in Toronto, Canada, in 1829. As a young girl, she moved with her family to Iowa. There she met and married Israel Mott, also a Canadian. Following their marriage, the entire Mott family moved to American Fork, Utah Territory, and in 1851 Eliza gave birth to Warren, her first child. Later that same year, the young Mormon couple left their infant with Israel's parents and became a part of the Western migration of Latter-Day Saints. They joined a Mormon emigrant train in Salt Lake and journeyed with them to Mormon Station, Nevada. There were several men, 18 women, and it is believed that the wagon train was led by Kit Carson. Eliza had all their belongings, including a cherrywood piano and her rocking chair, carefully packed in a wagon.

After several weeks of traveling over rough hazardous country, the small group arrived at the Carson Valley. While the oxen were being re-shod, Israel explored the valley and decided to remain there. The rest of the wagon train went on to California, and the Motts, who were farmers, proceeded south along the Carson River to the base of the Sierra Nevada. There, where a sparkling stream flowed down from the mountains, they decided to settle.

Eliza lived in the wagon, on the banks of the river, while Israel built their first house from abandoned wagon beds. He created a window sash with his jack-knife and found a piece of glass to fit it. Eliza became the first white woman to settle in the Carson Valley, and they became the first white family to build a home in the area. The rest of the Motts, including Eliza's son Warren, arrived a year later. Hiram Mott, Israel's father, took over leadership of the family.

The Mormons were known to be hard-working settlers, and Hiram kept his family together as they diligently worked on their 2,100-acre claim. The men and women built comfortable log houses, an irrigation system, and brought the first thrashing machine and grist-mill to the Carson Valley. In 1854 Eliza, who now had a secure home, gave birth to her second child, Louisa Beatrice. Louisa is said to have been the first white girl born in the valley.

Although Hiram was considered the head of the family, Eliza had a strong will of her own. More families settled in the area, and the need for a school became apparent, so Eliza decided to teach classes in her kitchen. It is quite possible that there was a clash between Hiram and Eliza at this point. As a member of the Mott family, she had to do chores, along with caring for a husband and two young children. However, Eliza obviously won the battle because she opened her own school in 1854 and became Nevada's first teacher.

Eliza's strenuous schedule included housekeeping, feeding the stock, and milking the cows. She had to rise before dawn, put on her bonnet, a big coat, a pair of boots, and wrap her feet in barley sacks to keep them warm. She would milk six or seven cows, then return to the house to cook breakfast for her family and hired hands. Next Eliza carefully prepared lunches for the students and then started her school day. Eventually another woman came in to assist the young woman with her teaching.

Later the school that began in a kitchen was replaced by a one-room frame building with plastered walls and two six-pane sash windows. It was named the Mottsville School, and a man named Austin became the first teacher. In the winter the children walked to school with their feet wrapped in barley sacks tied with a string. The first older boy to arrive had to start the fire, and the older girls were expected to clean and sweep the school at the end of each day. There were no indoor restrooms.

By 1856, in the community now known as Mottsville, Eliza had her third child, Mary Elizabeth. The child died in 1857, and Eliza, filled with grief, buried her daughter in the back yard of the Mott home. Later a neighbor's child died and was also buried there. These two graves were the start of what eventually became the Mottsville Cemetery.

Israel, in 1858, became one of the judges of the election in the Mottsville Precinct, and the first court was held in Mr. Mott's barn. The Motts also added the Tambourine Hall, a building for dancing and social events. They were no longer members of the Mormon faith.

Eliza and Israel had two more children, and in 1863 Israel died leaving Eliza with four children to raise. She married a neighbor, A. M. Taylor, in 1864, and her father-in-law, Hiram Mott, for the sum of $800, deeded 80 acres of the family claim to Eliza. Mr. Taylor and Eliza operated the ranch together. She continued to do the milking and added "a string of pigs." Eliza would set the milk in big milk pans every morning, and later she would skim off the cream to make butter and cheese. It was churned, placed in a mold, and then taken to Carson City to sell. The milk pans had to be washed and put in the sun for sterilization, and the rough boards of the kitchen floor were scrubbed by hand. There was no running water inside the home.

Eliza also kept a garden where she raised their vegetables. She did all the baking, cooked for the family, and made their clothing, along with straw hats for the men. Often late at night, Eliza would be summoned to help deliver a child and was recognized as a mid-wife. She always had time to help others.

Eliza wasn't like the modern woman, she never wore trousers. They were considered scandalous! While most of the women wore long dresses, Eliza always wore a short skirt and boots that reached the skirt at her knees. With this sensible type of clothing, it was easy to feed the stock and drive the wagon.

Entertainment consisted of music played on the cherrywood piano that Eliza brought with her across the plains. They would often go dancing at the Tambourine Hall and many times hitched up the buggy to attend a musical event in Virginia City. Eliza was also fond of playing cards, and she and Mr. Taylor enjoyed a good game almost every night. They had to play by candle light because Mr. Taylor was afraid of kerosene lamps.

In 1890 Mr. Taylor died, and Eliza, with the help of her sons Warren and George, continued to operate the ranch until her death.

In her later years, Eliza began to smoke a Meerschaum pipe with a short stem, and on occasion she even enjoyed a cigar. Eliza would prop her feet up by the fire and sit in the little rocker that was carefully carried in the wagon so many years before. Instead of a cuspidor, she used a small box filled with sand. It was unusual to see a woman of that era smoking a pipe or a cigar, but Eliza didn't care. She found they helped to ease the pain of her toothaches. Instead of driving over the hill to Placerville for a dentist, she smoked a pipe for relief.

In 1909, at the age of 86, Eliza Mott-Taylor quietly passed away. Her funeral was appropriately held in the Mottsville School. The Reverend Francis C. Ball offered a moving tribute to this sterling pioneer lady when he said in part: "I seldom if ever saw a more beaming face . . . . A friend by my side . . .said she did all the good that she could in every way she could wherever and to whomever she could! This out of the pure goodness of her heart without thought or hope of reward."

The Genoa Weekly-Courier, 1909, wrote: "A very large procession accompanied the remains to the cemetery, the Mottsville Cemetery near where she settled in those far-off, rigorous pioneer days, and there at the base of God's most majestic mountains, the Sierras, all that was mortal of this good woman, Mrs. Eliza Mott-Taylor, was tenderly laid to rest."

Courtesy of Beatrice Fettic Jones

Israel Mott, Eliza's husband.

Courtesy of Beatrice Fettic Jones

Mrs. Eliza Mott-Taylor at the age of 73.
Eliza's husband, Israel, passed away in 1863,
and in 1864 she married Mr. Taylor.

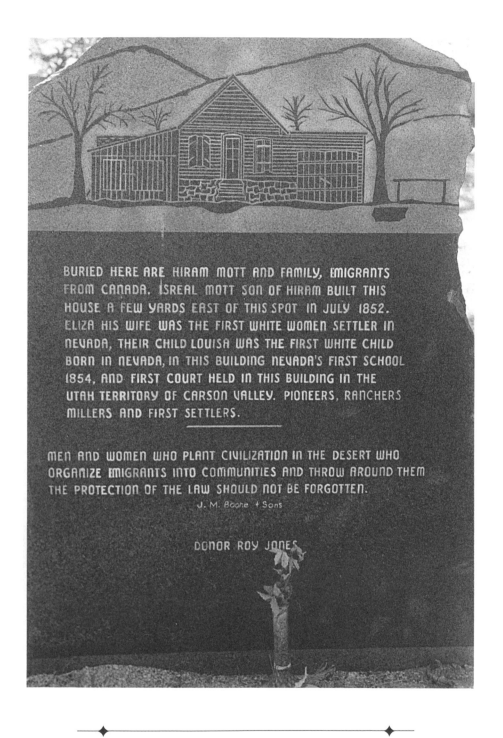

Mott family tombstone in the Mottsville Cemetary.

Courtesy of The Lake County Museum

◆━━━━━━━━━━━━━━━━━━━━◆

*The Kelsey Creek School, 1882, is a prototype of
most of the little western schoolhouses of the 19th-century.*

EARLY SCHOOLROOMS

Most of the schools of the Sierra in the 1800s were crude, inhospitable dwellings within mining camps and other small communities. They were usually made of logs, or adobe, with earthen floors, plastered walls, and, in some cases, thatched roofs. Many students sat upon wooden boxes, without desks, or a single desk would be shared by two pupils. The older students helped teach the younger ones, and the classes were not clearly defined. It was a rare school that had a piano or organ, so music was not always part of the curriculum.

All schools were cold in the winter, and the focal point of the room was the stove that sat in one corner. Lunch boxes (usually made from old tobacco tins), coats, and other necessities were kept in a small area known as the anteroom.

Pupils came from two or three miles away and arrived by horse, cart, or on foot. On cold days they wrapped their feet in sacks to provide warmth. Chores were required of each child. The boys fed and saddled the horses and kept the fire burning. The girls assisted the teacher and kept the classroom clean. When the temperature was low, the boys ate lunch outside, or in the woodshed, while the girls ate inside the room.

There was no indoor plumbing, and drinking water was kept in a pail with a dipper. If permission was needed to leave class, the child would raise his right arm, and only one child at a time was allowed to leave the room. There were two outhouses, one for each sex. They were freezing in the winter, and foul-smelling in the summer.

Fortunately, schools were greatly improved in the later part of the century when school districts became organized.

EARLY TEACHERS

In 1861, Hannah Clapp, an outspoken schoolteacher from Michigan, followed the silver boom to Carson City. She opened the first private school in Nevada, seven years after Eliza Mott started the first public school.

She was a tall, angular woman who wore tailored suits with a watchband suspended across her stomach. Her shoes were sensible and her hats plain. In a debate, Hannah's deep voice could be heard booming out over the others. She believed in women's rights and the Temperance Movement, and was not shy about letting others know how she felt.

Miss Clapp taught school with an assistant named Miss Babcock, who was the antithesis of the outgoing Hannah. Miss Babcock was dainty and slender, with a gentle voice. She remained in the background, maintaining the household and helping to teach the classes, while Hannah, the crusader, went about her business as a political figure.

This unusual pair taught kindergarten through twelfth grade, for 25 years, until Miss Babcock's death in 1899. Her death was a blow to Miss Clapp who donated $500 toward the Reno kindergarten so it would be known as the Babcock Memorial Kindergarten, and in 1908, she, too, passed away. Hannah Clapp's influence and contributions to education and woman's rights will always be remembered in the Carson area.

Teachers like Hannah Clapp and Miss Babcock, however, were the exception rather than the rule. In the early 1800s, teaching was a male-dominated occupation. Females did not have the opportunity to attend college, so they were unable to enter the field. It would seem that

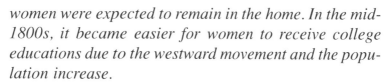

women were expected to remain in the home. In the mid-1800s, it became easier for women to receive college educations due to the westward movement and the population increase.

In the 1800s, the stereotype of a woman schoolteacher was that of an angular spinster, or a prim and proper young woman. In reality, teachers were just like other women and did not fit into a particular mold. Many of the ladies came from influential families in the east. Some were filled with missionary zeal, while a few were seeking a husband. Others migrated west because they were looking for a new future and were dedicated teachers.

They were underpaid and not considered professionals. The average salary was about $48 a month, less than half the wages paid miners for digging ore. From that meager amount of money, they were expected to pay room and board. When meals and lodging were included, the home was usually a barren log cabin providing only the bare essentials. Food, however, was plentiful and nourishing.

Conditions in the schoolrooms were primitive and uninviting. Teachers endured large classes with few textbooks. Somehow, this dedicated group survived despite the adverse conditions. Through determination and femininity, these women managed to change the social climate of the Sierra, and brought a degree of morality and education to the raw communities.

Courtesy of The Lake County Museum

Mrs. Langtry in "Lady of Lyons."

Chapter 6

LILLIE LANGTRY

America's First Superstar

O ne of the brightest stars to travel across the evening sky was that of the famous Lillie Langtry. She was a beautiful, unconventional actress and the most celebrated courtesan of the era.

Her light was destined to shine throughout three continents for almost 35 years. During that time, Lillie was proclaimed America's first superstar, touring the country from coast to coast. Her frequent appearances in the northern Sierra filled every theater. She was one of the most exciting actresses to grace the stage at Piper's Opera House.

Emilie Charlotte Le Breton was born in 1853, on the Isle of Jersey, off the coast of England. The Le Bretons had lived on this island almost a thousand years and, at one time, served the Norman Kings of England. Under the rule of Edward I, the family losing their wealth and property, turned to the professions and sea. Lillie's father, the Dean of the Isle of Jersey, was a tall, well-educated man with the presence of a natural leader. Lillie inherited an intense pride in her family heritage from him, and, as a Le Breton, she carried this pride throughout her life.

Emilie was given the nickname Lillie early in life. Growing up on the small Jersey island with six brothers for playmates, she learned to climb a cliff, ride a horse bareback, and fight like a boy before she was six years old. Educated by tutors, Lillie was undisciplined and lacked the proper social behavior.

Maturity arrived early for Lillie. Her body was well-developed at 14, and at 15 she received her first proposal of marriage from a 23-year-old lieutenant. When she confessed her age the stunned officer requested a transfer, and Mrs. Le Breton realized her daughter's need for an enlightening visit to England.

Ecstatic and filled with self-assurance, Lillie, who had never been off the small island, sailed with her mother to London. It was a trip that became a disaster for the unsophisticated girl and changed her life. The new island-made gowns she thought so stylish were not fashionable. She had never learned to dance or carry a conversation, and was bewildered by the large array of silverware at the dining table. Lillie survived by observing others and following their lead.

Defeated and humiliated, Lillie and her mother returned to the security of the Jersey Isle. Lillie held her head high and vowed she would someday return to conquer London and never again be disgraced. Putting yesterday aside, she spent the next few years studying literature and the art of social graces. At the end of this period, Lillie realized she had no special skills or training. She decided to marry a wealthy gentleman who would take her to London and provide a life of excitement and luxury.

Lillie, at 20, was an exceptionally beautiful and intelligent woman. She had an exquisite cameo complexion, sparkling violet-blue eyes, and long chestnut hair worn in a graceful knot at the nape of her neck. Taller than most women, Lillie's sensational wasp-waisted figure was envied by women and admired by men. Elegant and poised, she had acquired the rare gift of making everyone feel important.

When Edward Langtry sailed into the Jersey Harbor aboard his yacht, the "Red Gauntlet," he appeared to be all Lillie longed for: wealthy, educated, and handsome. Lillie later in life said she "fell in love with the yacht," and it was obvious Edward fell in love with her beauty. They were married as soon as possible, spending their honeymoon aboard the Gauntlet. However, this was not a marriage made in paradise. Edward was not as wealthy as Lillie was led to believe. He was an amiable, uneducated bumpkin who was content to spend his days on the yacht. He had no profession and showed little interest in one. Edward definitely did not fit into the lifestyle of Lillie's dreams for the future.

The first home the couple occupied was a large mansion near London. Lillie had no idea how to manage a household, and it is doubtful that she would have bothered had she known. Edward hired servants. Soon after the move Lillie contracted typhoid fever. The doctor predicted a long convalescence and felt she should return to Jersey. The strong-willed Lillie convinced him she would recover faster in London, so Edward rented apartments. The move almost caused bankruptcy.

Edward was bored and uncomfortable in London. He longed for the old days of sailing and the freedom of the Jersey Isle. Lillie spent her days reading and planning how she would be received into London society. Her future never looked brighter.

The death of Lillie's beloved younger brother brought a brief end to her happiness. Grief stricken, she returned from the funeral determined to wear only black. The Langtrys received their first invitation to a reception during her period of mourning. Edward, reluctant to attend, was persuaded by his wife to escort her for the sake of appearances.

Lillie owned no fashionable gowns or jewelry suitable for the affair, and Edward did not have the money nor the inclination to provide them. In desperation she lowered the neckline of a simple black dress and captured her bright hair in a single braid at the back of her neck. Lillie had achieved a vision of elegant simplicity that set her apart from the other women. The Langtrys entrance created a sensation.

John Millais, the famous artist, was immediately drawn to Lillie and declared her a Greek goddess. She promised to let him paint her portrait. Frank Miles, popular for his pen and ink illustrations, sketched her beauty in pencil. James Abbott McNeil "Jimmy" Whistler, offered his friendship to both Lillie and Edward. He was the only man present who took the time to make Edward feel comfortable.

Lillie became the center of attraction, disarming the women with simple honesty and capturing the men with her beauty. She was the toast of London.... "A Professional Beauty." Pictures of Lillie appeared overnight in shop windows throughout the city. This shocked the titled ladies because it was not acceptable; however, the unconventional Lillie loved it. Invitations to dinners, balls, dances and receptions flowed in. Oscar Wilde, author/dramatist, titled her "The Jersey Lillie," and wrote poetry describing her charm and loveliness. Lillie continued to wear black gowns. Edward Langtry, never comfortable with the aristocracy, began a career of drinking. He escorted his wife as custom demanded and retired into the background whenever possible. They no longer shared the same bedroom.

It was inevitable that Albert Edward VII, Prince of Wales, Queen Victoria's son and the future King Edward VII of England, would meet the exciting Mrs. Langtry, and they would become lovers. Their passionate, well-known but discreet affair continued off and on for almost three decades. His wife, the charming Princess Alexandra, politely turned the other way. Lillie was the first lover that "Bertie," the prince, openly acknowledged.

Their romance came to a temporary halt when the scandalous Lillie drank too much champagne and put ice down Bertie's neck at a gala affair. The Prince, furious at her public display of intimacy, stalked from the room leaving Lillie to fend for herself. Word spread throughout London that she received a direct social cut. Her devoted admirers disappeared and were replaced by creditors.

The Langtrys had been living far beyond their means, and Edward, in order to avoid a public auction of their belongings, tried in vain to raise money. Devastated, Lillie discovered she was pregnant, and returned to Jersey leaving her husband behind. It is uncertain whether the Prince came to Lillie's aid, taking her with him to France, or if the child was born in Jersey.

Jeanne Marie Langtry's birth was never certified or registered, and Mr. Langtry was not informed. Bertie never denied his paternity, although it has been written that Jean Marie's real father was Prince Louis Battenberg of Prussia. He was the favorite nephew to the Prince of Wales, and, later in life, he established the English branch of the family now known as Mountbatten. Lillie left Jeanne Marie with her mother who raised the child as Lillie's sister.

Determined to support herself, Lillie returned to London where her faithful friend, Oscar Wilde, helped shape her future. Wilde, famous for his wit, worshiped beauty and Lillie. He introduced her to Henrietta Hobson Labouchere, a noted drama teacher. In 1881, Lillie appeared in a charity performance of "She Stoops to Conquer." It was her first acting role, and the Jersey Lillie, who was now 28, became an instant success. Her popularity and theatrical ability began to earn money and fame. She toured Europe and was persuaded by Wilde to bring the theatrical group to the United States.

The first Western tour earned more money than Lillie dreamed possible. In America, however, her acting ability was considered secondary to her beauty and notoriety. She no longer wore black. Her gowns, cloaks, shoes, hats, and hairstyle became the vogue and were copied by the rich and poor alike. The girl who once had no fashionable gowns to wear now set the fashions. People ran after her on the street; she was surrounded by crowds wherever she went. Lillie loved it!

Judge Roy Bean, a bachelor from Vinegaroon, Texas, fell in love with Lillie's photographs and posters. He changed the name of the town to Langtry, covering the walls of his saloon with pictures and press clippings. Later in her life, Lillie visited the turn-of-the-century cow-town and was welcomed by the whole community. Always careful to be kind, Lillie treated the "proper ladies" and prostitutes with equal respect. She shook the women's hands and asked each "girl" her name. Lillie, the proper ladies, and the prostitutes, shared coffee and conversation together in the town post office. When Lillie departed, she was presented the late Judge Roy Bean's pistol...the same one used to keep order west of the Pecos, as well as in the "Jersey Lilly (sic) Saloon."

Lillie was America's first superstar, and was admired by famous writers like George Bernard Shaw, Walt Whitman, and Joaquin Miller. Her colleagues included distinguished stars such as Helen Modjeska and famed actress Sarah Bernhardt. Flamboyant Diamond Jim Brady showered Lillie with diamond trinkets. Wilde introduced her to a tall, well-known gentleman of fashion and leisure, Freddie Gebhardt. Freddie was seven years younger than Lillie and extremely handsome and wealthy. He was said to have been the real love of Lillie's life.

The dark-haired Freddie became Lillie's constant companion. They toured America in comfort aboard the "Lalee," a custom-made 75-foot luxury railroad car. The car was one of many gifts Freddie gave Lillie. It was painted bright blue with a wreath of golden lilies entwined on both sides.

In 1882, following a successful tour in San Francisco, Lillie made her first appearance in the Sierra. Leaving the Lalee behind, Freddie and Lillie traveled by special railroad car to Virginia City, where a large crowd awaited them at the station. When the handsome couple emerged from the train they were greeted by cheers, pelted by flowers, and whisked away to the International Hotel.

The evening of her first performance at Piper's Opera House was a special event for the local citizenry. They lined the streets attempting to catch a glimpse of the Jersey Lillie. Although many famous actresses had visited before, none were as notorious, or beautiful, as the star who was about to appear. Smiling and vibrant, Lillie stepped out of the hotel, waved to her admiring fans, and looked with dismay at the dusty uneven streets. They would destroy her expensive gown and slippers! She politely requested a carpet be laid from the hotel to the opera house. After a frantic search, the only carpet large enough happened to be red. Lillie received what is believed to be the first "Red Carpet" treatment. The famous stars who followed always insisted that the Red Carpet be spread for them as it was for the Jersey Lillie.

Lillie went on to appear in Carson City. She purchased land there which later yielded a rich vein of silver. Her next appearance was Tahoe City, where she fell in love with the beauty of the Sierra. She became a frequent guest of the wealthy Lucky Baldwin and spent many happy weekends at his estate. Lillie visited the Sierra many times in her career and always packed the theater. Her posters and portraits can still be found in the mining towns and cities of the area.

For many years, Lillie had attempted unsuccessfully to obtain a divorce from Edward Langtry. Although he would not consider divorce, he did accept the generous allowance she sent. In 1887, determined to be free of Edward, Lillie became a citizen of the United States, where the divorce laws were more liberal. She was the first woman to take out naturalization papers.

Once a citizen, Lillie decided to purchase a working ranch and establish a winery in the Guenoc Valley of Lake County, California. Freddie bought the adjoining property. Lillie loved her newfound paradise. The couple shared an interest in horse racing and decided to start a horse ranch. Freddie sent for 13 of his prize race horses. They were loaded on a train of 13 cars. The engine was number 13. On the 13th day of the month the horses were all destroyed in an accident. Whether it was superstition or loss of interest, the property was sold. Lillie's home, a California State Historic Landmark, and her vineyards have become a part of the Guenoc Winery. Her home and the winery are open to the public, and a cameo of the famous Jersey Lillie graces each bottle of Guenoc Winery's award-winning wine.

The love affair of Freddie and Lillie ended soon after the sale of their property. Bertie, who had never lost interest in Lillie, resumed his relationship with her. Their affection and friendship continued until his death.

Lillie received a divorce from Mr. Langtry in 1897, and a few years later shocked society when she married Sir Hugo de Bathe, a titled playboy 19 years her junior. Sir Hugo's father disinherited him because of the marriage. The wealthy Lillie, who could afford a husband, became the Lady de Bathe.

Their affection for each other did not last. Sir Hugo soon resumed his pursuit of younger women. Lillie, happy with her title, calmly continued her career and ignored her husband's indiscretions. In 1904, she scandalized America in the play, "Mrs. Derring's Divorce," where she dared to remove her clothing down to a full slip. Later she performed in vaudeville and moving pictures. When Lillie retired, in 1915, at age 62, she had achieved fame, a title, and was considered one of the richest women in the world.

On February 12, 1929, Charlotte Le Breton Langtry de Bathe died quietly in her home in Monaco. Lillie's last request was to be buried next to her parents on the Isle of Jersey. Her last words were "Is that you Freddie?"

The little tomboy who dared to conquer London and became the first lady of beauty and the theater was gone. She left memories, songs, and poetry that will live on. Although her star grows dim, it will never fade away.

Courtesy of The Lake County Museum

*Edward Langtry at the time of his marriage to Lillie.
In the latter part of his life Mr. Langtry was declared insane, and on
October 3, 1897, he died at the Cheshire County Asylum.*

From the private collection of Orville Magoon, Guenoc Winery

*Mrs. Langtry as Blanche Haye in the comedy "Ours,"
a play dealing with the Crimean War.*

EDWARDS' "HARLENE" FOR THE HAIR.

THE GREAT HAIR PRODUCER, RESTORER, AND DRESSING.

RESTORES, STRENGTHENS BEAUTIFIES, AND PROMOTES THE GROWTH OF THE HAIR.

PREVENTS ITS FALLING OFF AND TURNING GREY.

MRS. LILLIE LANGTRY,

The Charming Actress and Manager,

Writes: " Previous to my using HARLENE, my hair had become brittle and was falling off. I have used your preparation daily for 18 months, and my hair is quite restored.

" I cannot recommend Harlene too highly.

" Imperial Theatre, March 11, 1902."

1s., 2s. 6d., and (three times 2s. 6d. size) 4s. 6d. per Bottle from Chemists and Stores all over the World, or sent direct on receipt of Postal Order.

A FREE SAMPLE BOTTLE will be sent to any person filling up this Form and enclosing 3d. for carriage. If presented personally at our Offices no charge will be made.

Name...

Address...

ILLUSTRATED LONDON NEWS.

EDWARDS' "HARLENE" CO., 95 & 96, HIGH HOLBORN, LONDON, W.C.

From the private collection of Orville Magoon, Guenoc Winery

The Illustrated London news, May 3, 1902.

Courtesy of The Lake County Museum

Mrs. Langtry as Lady Ormonde in "Peril."

Courtesy of The Lake County Museum

Mrs. Langtry in the first act of "As You Like It."

From the private collection of Orville Magoon, Guenoc Winery

◆————————————————◆

Mrs. Langtry as Aphrodite in "A Society Butterfly,"
at the Opera Comique. June 20, 1894.

From the private collection of Orville Magoon, Guenoc Winery

◆━━━━━━━━━━━━━━━━━━━━━━◆

Mrs. Langtry in "Madamoiselle Mars."

Courtesy of The Lake County Museum

Mrs. Langtry as Juliet in "Romeo and Juliet."

Mr. Orville Magoon
Curator
Lillie Langtry Collection
PO Box 1146
Middletown, CA 95461

From the private collection of Orville Magoon, Guenoc Winery

First day of issue,
Lillie Langtry commemorative stamp, Isle of Jersey.

From the private collection of Orville Magoon, Guenoc Winery

◆————————————————————————————————————◆

Cameo of Lillie Langtry, painted by George Frederick Watts.
The cameo hangs above the fireplace in
Mrs. Langtry's home in Lake County, California.

From the private collection of Orville Magoon, Guenoc Winery

In the late 1800s a lady of Lillie's stature would never consider using her name for advertising. Lillie, however, did it for fun...and charged 132 pounds because that was how much she weighed.

Judge Roy Bean's "Jersey Lilly Saloon" in Langtry, Texas

From the private collection of Orville Magoon, Guenoc Winery

◆————————————————————————————◆

Judge Roy Bean was known as the "hanging judge," who fell in love with Lillie's photographs and posters. The judge changed the name of of the town from Vinagaroon to Langtry, and covered the walls of his saloon with pictures and press clippings of the famous Lillie.

Courtesy of The California State Libray

◆━━━━━━━━━━━━━━━━◆

*Lola Montez, about the time of her visit to New York.
Her vivid beauty and unorthodox relationship
to King Ludwig rocked the city.*

Chapter 7

LOLA MONTEZ
The Notorious Countess of Landsfield

Among the many fascinating personalities to stroll the dusty streets of Grass Valley, none was more exciting than Lola Montez. Her aura of mystery and wicked sensuality drove the miners wild.

"Notorious I have always been and never famous" were the words Lola used to describe herself. It has been said, Lola's misfortune was there was too much life in her to be held within the limits of one woman.

Eliza Gilbert was born in Ireland in 1818. She was the daughter of a Spanish beauty and a soldier in the British Army. Her father was transferred to India when Eliza was a baby, and she enjoyed a happy life until his sudden death. Her mother remarried, and Eliza was sent to live with Calvinistic relatives in England. The child missed her father and had a difficult time adjusting to the strict rules of her new environment.

When Eliza was in her early teens, her mother returned to England to arrange a marriage between the young girl and a 60-year-old judge of the Supreme Court of India. Eliza rebelled and, in despair, married a British lieutenant who was on his way to Bombay. Neither the lieutenant nor the rebellious Eliza were prepared for marriage, or ready to give up their personal relationships with others. Eliza eventually divorced her husband, claimed she was born in Spain, and changed her name to Lola Montez. As a child, her dancing had always been admired, so Lola decided to become a dancer. At first, she found it hard to convince the public she was from Spain...and even harder to make them believe she could dance. But soon that would all change.

Lola was a striking woman with a voluptuous bosom and tiny waist. Masses of dark curly hair circled a pretty face with black flashing eyes that captivated men of all ages. Lola had the ability to invent what she wanted and the power to convince others it was fact. Although her dancing skills were not outstanding, she gained access to most of the royal courts of Europe. Lola was always seen in the company of gentlemen of wealth and position, and she was considered a "fatal beauty."

While performing in a Munich theater, Lola met the lunatic King of Bavaria, Ludwig I, a sexagenarian who made her his mistress. Ludwig was so smitten with Lola that he gave her a fortune and let her control his country. Her politics, however, were as awkward as her dancing, and she made a shambles out of Bavaria. Ludwig eventually lost his crown and Lola was banned from the country. The King continued to send her an allowance, and Lola retained her title.

In St. Petersburg, Russia, Lola had a brief affair with His Imperial Majesty, Nicolas I. She then traveled on to Paris where Alexander Dumas fell madly in love with her. Lola fell in love with his best friend, journalist Alexander Dujarier. Dumas said later that "she had an evil eye and would bring a curse on any man who loved her."

In 1850, Lola became very ill and took many months to recover. She became weak and depressed. The allowance from Ludwig had stopped and creditors were knocking at her door. At 33, her career was not going well. Still determined to be famous, Lola decided to visit America, where she felt she could change her image and achieve success.

Lola sailed for America in 1851; unfortunately, her fame and notoriety had preceded her. When she arrived in New York City, she created an uproar and her first performances received bad reviews. She had fights with managers and lovers as she toured the country. The news media enjoyed it. The Countess of Landsfield, it seemed, could not change her image!

Lola's "Spider Dance" finally brought her a measure of success. In this dance, created in Europe, Lola would appear on stage wearing sheer flesh-colored tights with layers of chiffon circling her waist. The spiders were giant tarantulas made of cork so they would bounce. Lola would spin and whirl, rapidly flicking the spiders from her skirt, becoming more and more frantic as the dance went on. At the end, when she stamped the last arachnid, Lola would leap from one side of the stage to the other with her hands and feet spread before her like a large spider. It was a fantastic sight that both thrilled and shocked the audiences.

With the Spider Dance, Lola began to have successful tours throughout America. However, once the audience had seen the dance, she had nothing more to offer. She again began creating disturbances with her quick temper and entanglements with admirers.

In San Francisco, following a performance, she met the handsome Patrick Hull, publisher of the *San Francisco Whig*. Lola married him because he was the best story-teller she knew. The couple traveled the Sierra and decided to settle in Grass Valley. Lola was 35, newly-married, and tired of a career that was not going well. They bought a cottage on Mill Street and set up housekeeping. Today her home has been restored and is a state Historic Landmark, as well as the office of the Grass Valley and Nevada County Chamber of Commerce.

Lola was happy in the picturesque mining town of Grass Valley. It reminded her of Bavaria. Her home was lavish. Important personalities came from all over the world to visit the Countess. She lived high, smoked Cuban cigars, ate imported foods and drank the finest liquors. It was said she bathed in champagne and dried herself with rose petals. She also had a menagerie of animals, including a pet bear and a white parrot who perched on her shoulder. In her garden, Lola grew roses beside cactus plants.

Hull, who had writer's ink in his blood, missed his newspaper and wanted to return to San Francisco. Lola did not. One night, following a violent argument, she threw his suitcases out the window in a fit of rage. Hull left her for his newspaper, and that was the end of the marriage. The unconcerned Lola went on with her life...she shook off her husband as easily as she had her Irish ancestry.

Grass Valley in 1853, was the sixth largest town in California. The dusty unpaved streets were noisy both day and night. It did, however, have a theater on the second floor above the Alta Saloon. Lola appeared there for a brief time, but it was always the same pattern. The house sold out the first night to an enthusiastic audience; repeat performances were never well attended. She fared better in nearby Nevada City, but became discouraged and started having private shows for her friends. She always danced her signature, the Spider Dance.

Lola began traveling, and she took the time to entertain the lonely miners throughout the Sierra. She was a welcome sight as she went from camp to camp. The men appreciated the exciting Countess who shared more than her dancing with them. They loved Lola's performances and Lola!

But not all were in love with Lola. An editor of one of Grass Valley's newspapers wrote an article that displeased her. She attacked him verbally and attempted to hit him with a whip.

A methodist minister also condemned the Spider Dance, as well as the dancer. Lola was so angry she went to the minister's home, threw off her coat, and performed her dance in costume before the shocked man and his wife. The minister never mentioned the Countess of Landsfield, or her dance, in front of the congregation again.

Although Lola lived in Grass Valley for only two years, she played an important role in the area's past. She was a woman who was many things, depending on who did the viewing. People were important to Lola. She befriended little Lotta Crabtree, taking time to teach the child many intricate dance steps. Lotta went on to fame... Lola never did.

Lola left Grass Valley for a tour of Australia where her performances were a disaster. In desperation, Lola offered herself as a repentant sinner appearing in a series of religious lectures. Most of the people who came were curious, not in need of salvation. She returned to New York, her body weak and wasted and the electrifying sparkle missing from her eyes. Lola attempted a new lecture tour; however, in her weakened condition, the strain was too much. She moved to Brooklyn where she had a stroke that left her unable to speak.

In a squalid boarding house in the Hell's Kitchen district of New York, Lola Montez died on January 17, 1861. The notorious Countess of Landsfield, once loved for her beauty and character...not her dancing...was only 42. Her lifetime had been a fable...with a little truth mixed in.

Courtesy of The California State Library

◆━━━━━━━━━━━━━━━━━━━━◆

Lola Montez and the "Spider Dance."
The dance was criticized, but it made her famous.

Courtesy of The California State Library

◆————————————————◆

*Lola Montez. She owed her popularity
more to the prestige of her name than any real talent.*

Courtesy of The California State Library

Potrait of Lola Montez, engraved by Auguste Hussner.
Lola was 30 years old at the time,
and she was married to a man who was 21.

Courtesy of The California State Library

◆━━━━━━━━━━━━━━━━━━━━━━◆

Lola Montez, in 1848. She was not considered a real artist,
however, she was the favorite of kings.

LOLA MONTEZ AND HER CIGARETTE

That somewhat eccentric lady, to say nothing harsher of her, was riding in a railroad car, when, notwithstanding notices placarded in the car, "No Smoking Allowed Here," she took out a cigarette, and was puffing at it very composedly when the conductor came along. He looked at her in astonishment, and finally, with some hesitation, addressed her.

"You can't smoke in here, Madame," he said.

"But you see I can," was the imperturbable reply, the cigarette removed just long enough to say the words, and then replaced, while Lola went on with her smoking the same as before.

The conductor, taken aback at the coolness of her reply, hesitated a moment, and then passed on, leaving the fair smoker to the enjoyment of her cigarette.

— *What Women Should Know, 1868*
By Mrs. E. B. Duffey

EARLY ENTERTAINERS
AND THEATERS OF THE WEST

Everyone likes to be entertained. The arrival of a theatrical troupe or a famous personality has always been exciting, and the early days of the West were no exception. Entertainers were always a welcome sight, especially in the mining towns and camps of the Mother Lode where the audience was mostly masculine. The miners wanted pleasing performers, and they were happy to reward them.

The early entertainers were a hardy group. They traveled long, uncomfortable miles over rugged mountains, dangerous trails, and arid deserts to see the glitter of gold and to achieve fame.

Once the actors and actresses reached their destination, they often had to perform under primitive conditions. There were no dressing rooms or sanitary facilities. Many times their stage would be the floor of a blacksmith's shop with a wagon canvas for a curtain. They would appear in a tent, schoolroom, or a saloon. The orchestra was usually a flute, violin, and guitar played by musicians who had never read a note.

They offered medicine shows, drama, and variety. There were special rooms with cheap decorations, where the patrons could meet an actress for a price. Many times a miner would pay $100 for a seat and toss more gold on the floor when the show was over.

In the early 1860s, theaters began to appear in the larger communities and cities. One of the first was The Downieville National Theater which was opened in 1860. It had a lofty ceiling, a deep stage for scenic effects, and a $600 chandelier.

In Virginia City, the Queen of the Comstock, the first theater, opened in 1860. It was called the Howard Street Theater and ladies were not admitted. Business was good so Maguire's Opera House opened its doors in 1863. It was an opulent establishment. The auditorium was carpeted, ornate crystal chandeliers hung from the ceiling, spectators were seated upon gilt chairs, and there were velvet railings for the boxes. The enthusiastic audiences were wealthy, but not necessarily elite. They came for entertainment and had the money to pay for it. The shows ranged from Adah Isaacs Menken in the "Mezeppa" to minstrels and dog fights.

John Piper acquired the opera house in 1868 and changed its name to Piper's. The theater went through a series of architectural changes and became one of the finest in the land. Piper brought in fresh new talent adding top entertainment. A few of the famous to appear were Lillie Langtry, Lotta Crabtree, Lillian Russell, Enrico Caruso, and comedian Eddie Foy and movie great, Marie Dressler.

Although the days of the traveling minstrels are gone, Piper's Opera House is still in operation as a theater and museum. Visitors will find old billboards announcing famous stars from the past, along with pictures and memorabilia from 100 years ago that are still very much alive today.

Courtesy of The California State Library

Lovable Lotta Crabtree...the child "Fairy Star" of the Sierra.

Chapter 8

LOTTA CRABTREE
America's Lovable Comedienne

Perched upon a makeshift table in the shade of the blacksmith shop, a pretty little moppet danced an Irish jig. The friendly miners, who had gathered to watch, were eager to be entertained. Little did they know they were watching the first steps of a future star.

The miners leaned against the walls as they drank and cheered the young dancer. The child tossed her bright red curls and delighted the men with her infectious laughter. Her nimble feet never missed a beat to the rhythm of the clapping hands.

The child was Lotta Crabtree...a Fairy Star. She was one of the talented youngsters who traveled the Sierra in the mid 1800s, entertaining the miners who missed the families they left behind. For one brief moment, this child with her rosy wholesome face reminded them of their own daughters. And the lonely men, often with tears in their eyes, were always generous at the end of each performance.

Charlotte Mignon Crabtree was born in New York in 1847. Her mother, Mary Ann Livesley, came from a proud, middle-class English family who earned its living by making upholstery and slip covers. Her father, John Ashworth Crabtree, also of English decent, was an easy-going, well-dressed bookseller. He was a charming man who enjoyed leisure far more than tending the store. Mary Ann was forced to continue working in the family business.

The discovery of gold in California, and the tales of instant riches, caught John Crabtree's interest. In 1851, he sold the bookstore, kissed his wife and child goodbye and headed west with a promise to send for them soon. Months later, Mary Ann received a message to meet her husband in San Francisco. She gathered little Lotta and her belongings and set out to join him. They traveled the perilous route around Cape Horn, and, when they arrived, John Crabtree was nowhere in sight. He had moved on!

Mary Ann, alone in the city with a small child to care for, managed to find lodging with friends. It was there Lotta saw the traveling child actors and actresses, and Mary Ann learned how much money they earned. She enrolled Lotta in her first dancing class.

John Crabtree, after many months of prospecting, had not found gold. He purchased a boarding house, located his family, and moved them to Grass Valley. Mary Ann took over the business of cooking, cleaning and caring for the miners. The notorious Lola Montez, who was also a resident of the mining community, became a friend of the family. She took a special interest in little Lotta and spent many hours teaching the child to dance. She also taught her to ride horseback, and the two of them became a familiar sight as they rode the many trails in the area.

Unfortunately, John Crabtree decided to move on to greener pastures. John, Mary Ann, and Lotta traveled from place to place, finally settling in La Porte, where Mary Ann once more became a reluctant housekeeper for the unwashed, dusty miners. She also met Matt Taylor, musician and dancer, who managed a saloon and small log theater where the traveling players often appeared.

Taylor felt Lotta had talent and took her under his supervision. With his help, the child's dancing ability and charm began to attract attention. Lotta's command of intricate steps and complicated rhythms, along with her bubbling love of life, was impressive. Mary Ann recognized her child's potential as an actress and decided to make a change. While Crabtree was in the mountains prospecting, she left him a note and a pot of beans and joined a traveling troupe. Matt Taylor was the director.

Lotta was almost eight years old, and looked more like six. As the troupe traveled by night from camp to camp, they strapped the child to the back of a mule. Lotta remembered her days on horseback with Montez and was not afraid. She even learned to sleep in the saddle. Their new home became a log hotel, tent, a flimsy canvas boarding house, or a place on the ground to throw a blanket.

Lotta danced her way through the mining towns and camps. Her performances were followed by the ring of gold nuggets, quarters, and valuable trinkets. The little redhead would quickly gather them up and put them in her shoe. Mary Ann became Lotta's manager, as well as investor, and the earnings were carefully put away for safe keeping.

John Crabtree joined the traveling troupe for a brief visit, and a few months later another baby was born. Lotta had her first brother. With two children to care for, Mary Ann depended more than ever on Lotta to provide for all of them. And she did! The troupe would enter a town with Taylor in the lead beating a big drum. They appeared in barrooms, basements, tents, small theaters, or any place that was available. Mary Ann also began to perform occasionally under the name of Miss Arabella. They were known as the Metropolitan Company, and although robberies were common in the Sierra, the little group managed to remain untouched.

As time moved on, more actors entered the arena; competition became intense. Wagon shows roamed the mountains offering burlesque, women dancers, circus acts, and a few well-known San Francisco actors. The days of the Fairy Stars were almost over, and the Metropolitan Company was forced to follow the mood of the audience. Lotta kept her head high above the ordinary entertainers. She could stand in the middle of a tiny stage with her robust laugh, and the whole room full of miners would join in. She learned Negro soft-shoe dancing and appeared in blackface, adding minstrel songs. She romped her way into the heart of the audience and became the pet of the miners.

The severe and upright Mrs. Crabtree used her skills to the utmost as she created new costumes for Lotta's many quick changes. She was still an attractive woman with high color and fine eyes, and, as Miss Arabella, won her share of the applause. The little troupe went on and on from camp to mining town, returning to San Francisco in the early winter where Lotta would study voice and piano. The Crabtree's still hoped for the legitimate theater.

Lotta was finally given an engagement in a bit theater called the "Gaieties"...a shabby place on the San Francisco waterfront surrounded by cheap businesses. This was the beginning of Lotta's experience in the variety field. She was accepted at "Maguire's Opera House" and was the youngest member of the cast. She played at the "What Cheers," "Gilbert's," the "Apollo," and the "Bella Union." She was billed as "La Petite Lotta," "Miss Lotta, the Unapproachable," and "Miss Lotta, the San Francisco Favorite."

Every theater had a bar, so Mrs. Crabtree always whisked Lotta in and out as fast as possible. Lotta was never allowed to join in the lively offstage parties, although she was reaching the age where a small diversion would have been a break in the girl's rigorous routine. She often had several performances on the same night at different theaters, and many times she became deeply depressed before going on stage. Mary Ann always managed to cheer the girl up. Once on stage, Lotta became a bundle of fresh life and mirth. It was as though all the unused capacity for social contacts and pleasures were poured out upon the stage.

The famous Adah Menken briefly entered Lotta's life. Mary Ann, flattered by the popular actress's attention, let Lotta and Menken become friends. They attended the races and visited other performers. Adah Menken also taught Lotta to smoke the long black cigars that became a trademark and part of Lotta's act.

Miss Lotta at 17 wore hoop-skirts and little round hats turned up behind. In burlesque, she could roll off a sofa, show more than a slim ankle, and be hilarious. Her skirts were daring, her smoking on stage in masculine parts were new to Lotta and comical. In the fight for top billing, she fought with all the vitality her small body could gather.

Although Lotta had many successes, and a reputation as a fine actress in the West, Mary Ann wanted Lotta to expand to greater heights. The girl had been singing and dancing for ten years without a break. Mrs. Crabtree was thrifty and invested Lotta's money well...so well, that Lotta did not own a silk dress until she was 21. They had what was considered a small fortune; with this in mind, the family, including John Crabtree, left for New York.

The New York critics were not as easy to please as the critics in San Francisco. Lotta, although a valuable star, was informed that her style was not intended for first-class audiences; she belonged in concert halls. Lotta began to creep into minor engagements with a third-rate manager. She performed in Philadelphia, Pittsburgh, Cincinnati, Louisville, Buffalo, and the smaller towns of the midwest, accepting whatever she could find. It was a traumatic experience, and Lotta, who had difficulty learning her roles, was reluctant to appear. It was as though her spirit were broken. Lotta frequently forgot her lines on stage, so Mary Ann and Crabtree helped by filling in. Gradually, as Lotta's stock of plays increased, her confidence returned. She found she could perform as many as six roles in a single play. Once more she swaggered and romped her way through the parts. Raves followed, and she played the biggest houses to delighted audiences. Lotta was a star...and Crabtree finally found his gold mine; IT WAS LOTTA.

Mary Ann discouraged close relationships, so marriage was out of the question for Lotta. The news media carried occasional stories about her romances, but the men involved were merely friends and companions. Lotta's love of the theater and devotion to her mother came before any love she might have felt for a man. She was adored by all and showered with gifts...but lacked personal companionship. A new play, "Little Nell and the Marchioness," became the vehicle that carried Lotta to even greater heights. It was an extravaganza where she appeared so ethereal that the audience was reduced to tears. Lotta, however, did not like sadness or tears. She preferred the comic, saucy hoyden parts where her daring pantomime, her smoking, and her short skirts were shattering traditions. She became America's first comedienne. The audiences loved her and said she was like no other star.

Money rolled in, and the generous Lotta spent a great part of it on her family. Her brothers were sent to fine schools, and Mary Ann took Lotta to Paris for a vacation where Lotta learned to paint...a hobby that became a special part of her life. The Crabtrees also visited England where Lotta performed in the best theaters.

When the holiday was over, Mary Ann Crabtree quit the stage and retreated to wearing black with a dark shawl and bonnet. Her youth was gone. But, Lotta plunged into bolder and livelier performances. She delighted the audience with daring antics, impersonations of celebrities, and sentimental songs. She also began to appear in charity benefits, and in 1875, she presented a 35-foot cast-iron statue to the city of San Francisco. It was located at the intersection of Kearney and Market Streets and represented her appreciation for the city she loved (and who loved her).

Lotta spent her days painting and riding horseback over the countryside. She retained her girlish figure and sparkling brown eyes. When Mary Ann died in 1905, she left Lotta with a fortune and broken heart. Lotta declared she owed her entire career to her mother. Perhaps the devotion—the common bond that linked mother and daughter...was too close. In her grief, Lotta had a stained glass window placed in St.

Stephen's Church in Chicago as a token of her love.

In the last days of Lotta's life, she was very much alone. Purchasing a hotel in Boston, she catered to actors and the theater. Lotta appeared to need as many people around her as possible and was often seen wearing her costumes from earlier years. At other times, she would retreat to New Jersey where she would paint in solitude.

Lotta passed away in 1924 at the age of 77. The little moppet, who had no personal relationships and few associations, left her estate...estimated to be valued at $4 million....to strangers. She requested that her money be left to a foundation for the relief of needy veterans of World War I, hospitals, an actors' relief fund, students of music and agriculture, and for humane treatment of animals.

Members of her family, and strangers who pretended to be related, contested her Will. The court proceedings went on for years. The ring of Lotta's coins and glitter of her gold was audible throughout the trial. In the end, Lotta had her way...the Will remained unbroken.

Courtesy of the Searls Historical Society

The "Lotta" Cigar advertisement.

Courtesy of The California State Library

Lotta Crabtree.
She was loved by all, but lacked personal relationships.

Courtesy of The Nevada Historical Society

Lotta Crabtree in her early 30s.

Courtesy of The Nevada State Historical Society

"La Petite Lotta."

Lotta - Ma - and Shiftless Pa

Lotta, Ma, and shiftless Pa
All went to Rabbit Creek.
They n'er came back to Mill Street Shack
　　　So Lola Montez grew sick.
　　　While in such spell she left the dell,
　　　('Tis confidential truth)
　　　And rode all night with moon for light
　　　On black mare known as "Ruth."

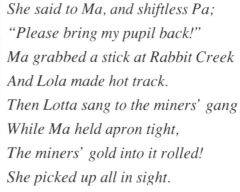

　　　She said to Ma, and shiftless Pa;
　　　"Please bring my pupil back!"
　　　Ma grabbed a stick at Rabbit Creek
　　　And Lola made hot track.
　　　Then Lotta sang to the miners' gang
　　　While Ma held apron tight,
　　　The miners' gold into it rolled!
　　　She picked up all in sight.

At last one day Ma hooked the bay
To the buckboard 'tween each thill.
Whence Lotta and Ma left shiftless Pa
And Drove down the hill.

Courtesy of The Nevada State Historical Society

From the private collection of Shirley Taylor.
(this picture is not to be reproduced without written consent from Shirley Taylor)

◆ ——————————————————————— ◆

Amelia Jelmini Celio at the time of her marriage to Frank Celio.
Amelia was 21 years old.

Chapter 9

AMELIA CELIO

A Gentle Woman

For almost a century, from 1853 to 1950, the Celio family owned and operated one of the largest enterprises in the Sierra. Their sawmills provided lumber for most of the homes built in the South Lake Tahoe area, and they were also responsible for the community's milk, butter, cheese and meat, and owned Meyers Station.

In 1892, Amelia Jelmini joined the prestigious pioneer family when she married Frank Celio. Through her gentle nature and dedicated work, Amelia became known as "the rock of the family."

Amelia Jelmini Celio was born in Amador County in 1871. As she grew up, she became a tall, slender woman with blond hair, firm sensitive features, and quiet brown eyes. Her pleasant personality attracted Frank Celio, and, after a brief courtship, they were married in 1892 at Placerville. Both were of Swiss ancestry.

Following the marriage, Amelia, who was 21, cheerfully assumed the duties of being a member of the Celio family. They moved into the home at "King's Store Ranch" called the Lower Ranch, located between Placerville and Plymouth. This was the first holding of Frank's father, Carlo Celio, who purchased the parcel in 1850 for $300 in gold coins. The second ranch in Lake Valley, Upper Ranch, was purchased in 1863 and was approximately 800 acres.

By the time Amelia married Frank, the Celios had established a pattern for the family that continued through the years. They would pasture their cattle at Upper Ranch during the summer, and by mid-October, they would be on the trail to Lower Ranch to move the cattle away from the heavy snow.

Every member of the family participated in the annual cattle drive. In the fall they would spend several days preparing for the trek over Echo Summit. There was bread to bake, food to store, and clothing to be packed. They took all their belongings with them...it was a big job.

Amelia made her first cattle drive a few months after her marriage. In June they started getting ready for the trip to the Upper ranch, and it must have been a strenuous ordeal for the new bride. She baked, cooked, and filled the "ticks" with hay. A "tick" was a mattress that was split down the center for easy storage, and served as a bed for the nights on the trail. On the day of the drive, Amelia took her place in one of the horse drawn wagons, and they headed for Lake Valley.

The first trip was an exciting event for the young woman. It took five or six days to reach the Upper Ranch. They went through Diamond Springs, up over Sacramento Hill, down the Main Street of Placerville, and on to Smith's Flat. There they settled in for the night and cooked dinner. The next stops were Pacific House, then Kyburz, and on to what once was Phillips' Station. By the end of the drive, everyone was exhausted; and Amelia had completed the first of many cattle drives she was to make over the years. On the return trip in October, she was expecting her first child. By then she had learned to kill a chicken, clean it, and cook it along the side of the trail. In 1902, her third child, Hazel, made the cattle drive at two months old, wrapped in a blanket in a basket on the seat of the buggy.

The home at Upper Ranch had no conveniences. It was a barren place until Amelia arrived. She brought a fresh new look to the old homestead, as well as a happy outlook on life. She worked from before sunrise to sunset cooking, cleaning, and helping with the milk and butter. The family raised beef and cattle and sold butter, cream, and eggs commercially. There were 80 cows that Amelia helped milk by hand. She also prepared the meals for the family and ranch hands, and washed clothes in a wash house with water carried from a creek. Amelia's congenial personality and gentle ways made everyone love her. The house was filled with laughter whenever she was there.

Her pleasures were simple. Amelia enjoyed making furniture for her home; many of her pieces are still in the "new house" the Celios built in 1914. Her other loves were flowers and working in her beautiful garden. There Amelia felt she could communicate with God; and alone, under the sky, she found her own religion.

Amelia never wore trousers or hats. She preferred simple dresses with homemade petticoats, and, on special occasions, she would add a little fancy lace. For work days and cattle drives, Amelia wore boots.

Saturday was the highlight of the week when Frank would take

Amelia dancing at Globin's Dance Hall on the shore of Lake Tahoe. That was the one night they shared alone, away from the routine of the ranch.

In 1903, the Celios purchased Meyers Station, and the family operated the hotel, dining room, blacksmith shop, cooperage, and general merchandise store for more than 35 years. Amelia adjusted her schedule to help in that venture, too.

Frank Celio passed away in 1923, leaving his share of the corporation known as C. G. Celio and Sons to Amelia. She attempted to carry on the firm as well as the family traditions. In 1950, five years before the expiration date of the corporation, the members of the family sold all their holdings. It was a sad day for the family.

As Amelia grew older, she spent more time with her grandchildren, and each one was special to her. She and her granddaughter Shirley, would get in her 1927 Chevrolet and go on a yearly picnic, something that became an important part of both their lives.

In 1958, when she was 87, Amelia Jelmini Celio died, leaving fond memories of a gentle, caring woman. A portion of the Upper Ranch was passed on in 1985 to her beloved granddaughter Shirley Taylor, who "feels she has been blessed with a vision to preserve what is left." Within ten years she plans to improve the land and have it looking like a park. Through Shirley Taylor, the Celios of the Sierra still live on.

From the book, I Remember, courtesy of The El Dorado Chamber of Commerce

◆━━━━━━━━━━━━━━━━━━◆

Frank E. Celio, husband of Amelia Celio
and father of Florance, Norman, and Hazel Celio.
Frank was born in Placerville in 1862.

From the book, I Remember, courtesy of The El Dorado Chamber of Commerce

Pictured from the left are, Hazel Celio, her mother Amelia, her father Frank, and brother Norman. Others are Carrie and Camilla Heald and Henrietta Celio.

Courtesy of Shirley Taylor

*The original Celio homestead at Upper Ranch with
Amelia Celio standing on the porch.*

◆━━━━━━━━━━━━━━━━━━━◆

*The new Celio ranch-house, built in 1914,
established in 1863.*

Courtesy of Shirley Taylor

*A Celio hay wagon traveling over Kingsbury Grade,
Nevada, in the year 1900.*

New York Public Library   *Courtesy of The El Dorado County Historical Museum*
THE COACHMAN WAS A LADY

Chapter 10

CHARLOTTE "CHARLEY" PARKHURST
◆ Stage-Driver (Jehu) ◆

S he chewed tobacco, smoked "two-bit" cigars, and was one of the best "whips" in the West. Her name was Charlotte "Charley" Parkhurst, a woman who, for reasons of her own, masqueraded as a man for almost 50 years.

Charlotte Darkey Parkhurst was born around 1812 in New Hampshire. She was placed in a Massachusetts orphanage at an early age and grew up surrounded by poverty and a lack of love. When Charlotte was about 15, she borrowed male attire and ran away from the institution disguised as a young boy. Since all the children's hair was cut short, it was easy to pass as a male. Charlotte obviously discovered that life was much less difficult for men than for women, so she decided to masquerade as a man the rest of her life. She adopted the name of Charles D. Parkhurst, and eventually became known as "Charley."

In Worchester, Massachuesetts, Charley applied for work at the stables of Ebenezer Blach and was hired immediately. She proved to be a diligent employee, cleaning stables, pitching hay, and caring for the horses. In return, Charley received room, board and low wages. She was fond of horses and learned how to handle a team. Charley became proficient with the reins and was considered one of the most popular drivers.

When her employer moved his business to Rhode Island, Charley went with him. There her instinctive talent and skill with the horses earned Charley the title of "Whip." She met two wealthy men who later started one of the first and largest gold-rush transport businesses. They invited Charley to move west.

Charles D. Parkhurst arrived in California in the early 1850s, and soon became known throughout the Sierra as a fearless stagecoach driver, "Jehu." She rode with such famous whips as Hank Monk, Charlie Crowell, and Jared Crandall. The early trails of California were no place for a lady...and nobody ever accused her of being one. Her face was weathered by sun and wind, and brown tobacco stains, from the large chaw she always had in her cheek, could be seen on her chin.

Charley was of medium build and height, with a voice that could be described as a "whiskey tenor." She had broad shoulders and was clean shaven with a scraggly moustache. She wore pleated blousy shirts (no doubt to hide her femininity) with wide belts. Her trousers were expensive, as were her buffalo skin coat, fancy high-heeled boots, broad Texas hat, and the embroidered buckskin gloves which covered her small, but strong hands. The gloves were necessary for the task of handling the teams on her long runs. They cost $20, and she seldom removed them...even for meals.

It could be said that she "cut a fancy figure." But if any of her male companions noticed her attire, they refrained from being critical because Charley could and would fight. A swift uppercut to the nose, a hard kick in the shins, and a strong right to the jaw were all that was needed. If this weren't enough, Parkhurst was also proficient in using a long blacksnake whip. At 15 paces, she could cut a cigar out of a man's mouth or slice the end off an envelope. The lady could definitely handle herself in barroom brawls.

Charley lost most of her feminine looks when an obliging horse kicked her in the eye. She was deprived of her sight in the eye and started wearing a black patch. She also gained the name of "One-eyed Charley."

Charley had many adventures while driving the trails of the Sierra during the gold-rush years. Once, when she was racing along, the team suddenly veered off the road, and she was thrown from the coach. Hanging on to the reins, she was dragged along and eventually managed to turn the runaway team into some bushes. The passengers showed their appreciation by presenting her with $20.

Although Parkhurst drove like a person possessed and would extend her team and passengers to the limits of their endurance, she was still a popular whip. Her rides were hair-raising, but Charley had a feel for the road that brought her through safely. On many occasions she would cover 60 miles a day on roads knee-deep in mud or water, and make the return trip as well.

One of her adventures in the gold country happened when a bandit ordered her to "throw down the box." The box was a Wells Fargo box which, no doubt, contained gold or coins. Charley, who was caught unprepared, threw the box down and learned a valuable lesson. From that time on, she carried her six-shooter on the seat beside her. The next time Charley heard someone repeat the same command, she grabbed her gun, fired into the bushes, and killed a notorious highwayman. This, obviously, ended her problems, because Charley did not have to kill another man.

Charley never boasted about her experiences, but others told of her skill. She was such an expert driver that she could run both wheels of her stagecoach over a quarter lying in the road with her horses going at top speed. She did all of this with only one eye! Parkhurst was such a fearless driver that when asked how she could see through the clouds of dust, she said, "I listen for the wheels to rattle...then I know I am on hard ground. If they don't rattle, I look to see if the road is there!" Then she would either chew on her cigar or spit tobacco.

With all of her masculine traits, Charley was not a heavy drinker. She was afraid of revealing her secret. She didn't care for gambling, except to shake the dice for cigars. Charley always carried candy for the children in her pocket, beside her chaw of tobacco. She was civil, but aloof, and lived a lonely life with no close friends. The other whips said of her: "He understood his business, he was pleasant and stiddy and sober. And with them, any feller can do well." She was accepted as a male and very much "one of the boys."

At the end of a trip, Charley would head for the stables to sleep with her horses. She had to keep to herself and that meant bunking alone. When razzed by the other Jehu, she would mutter that she seemed to get along better with horses than with people.

For all her gruffness, Parkhurst was a person who cared about others. She helped women in childbirth, set broken bones, and donated money to needy children. When a widow and her attractive daughter nearly lost their home due to lack of money, Charley bought the property and gave it back to the widow. In return, the woman wanted Charley to wed her daughter, and Charley left in a hurry. This puzzled the woman's friends who couldn't understand why "he" left the attractive woman behind.

Women were a problem. Many venturesome females insisted upon riding with this "Prince of Ribbons." They wore fashionable hoop-skirts and popular Shaker bonnets to hide their blushes when around Charley. All admired "Silent Charley" as "he" sat upon the seat dressed in "his" fancy attire. Every moment was exciting to the tittering ladies as Charley controlled the six lines, including the whip. Around the turns she would go, cussing at the horses, spitting tobacco, and, no doubt, secretly laughing at the foolish, admiring women. Needless to say, Charley seldom stayed in one place long.

Although Charley swore at the horses and slashed her whip, she took excellent care of her "babies;" no driver ever loved his horses more than Charley. Any whip who abused his animals would have her to reckon with.

With the end of the gold-rush years, Charley decided to retire. She had been driving the frontier stage for 15 years and stepped down from her coach to buy a stage station and saloon. It was located on the road between Watsonville and Santa Cruz, and Charley became a genial host...or hostess! Tiring of that, she moved to Soquel where she raised cattle.

There were two things Charley enjoyed discussing...horses and the obligation and right of every citizen to cast his ballot and vote. And, on November 3, 1868, at the age of 57, Charles Darkey Parkhurst, occupation farmer, from New Hampshire, cast her vote in the National Election. She became the first woman to vote in the United States, 52 years before the passing of the 19th Amendment. Charley also joined the order of the Odd Fellows and became an active member.

By 1876, at age 64, Charley was plagued with painful rheumatism. She sold her ranch and moved into a small cabin on the property of a friend, Mr. Harmon. There, with the help of a hired man and the friend's son, she managed to keep her secret while living out her last years. The young Harmon boy was kind to Charley, and she became fond of him.

Charley developed a persistent sore throat in 1879. Rather than visit the doctor, she treated herself like she did her horses...with patent remedies...none of which worked. Her ailment became worse, and when she finally saw the doctor, Charley had developed cancer of the throat and tongue. The many years of smoking and chewing tobacco had taken their toll. Her voice became a whisper, and she only conversed to express her various needs. In December, 1879, she passed away, leaving her estate to the Harmon boy.

As she was being prepared for burial, her secret was discovered—Charley Parkhurst was a well-endowed woman! Her best friend was mortified and greeted her death with profanity. The community was shocked and wondered how she could have fooled them for so many years. There were all kinds of comments and discussions. A postmortem examination was said to have shown that at one time Charlotte had given birth to a child. This brought on speculation that she once had an unfortunate love affair. It was also said that among Charley's personal things they found a red dress and a pair of baby shoes.

Why Charlotte posed as a man, only Charley knew; she took that secret with her to the grave. Regardless of her sex, Charley Parkhurst was a Jehu and one of the most fearless, skillful whips of the exciting gold-rush era!

"Charley"

CHARLEY DARKEY PARKHURST
1812 — 1879

NOTED WHIP. OF THE GOLD RUSH DAYS
DROVE STAGE OVER Mt. MADONNA IN
EARLY DAYS OF VALLEY. LAST RUN
SAN JAUN TO SANTA CRUZ. DEATH IN
CABIN NEAR THE 7 MILE HOUSE,
REVEALED "ONE EYED CHARLIE",
A WOMAN. THE FIRST WOMAN TO VOTE
IN THE U. S. NOV. 3, 1868

ERECTED 1955

PAJARO VALLEY HISTORICAL ASS'N.

Courtesy of The El Dorado Historical Museum

Courtesy of El Dorado Historical Museum

◆ ──────────────────────────────────── ◆

Hank Monk
Charley drove stage with famous drivers like Hank Monk,
who was considered to be the world's greatest reinsmen.

THE JEHU

"The fearless and sure Jehu safely guides the highest nettled horses, those untamed broncos of a Spanish sire and dam, with the lives of sometimes 19 passengers resting easily in the palm of his clenched hand, the flick of his whip, or the multiple reins. No matter how stormy the night, how long, dark or dreary, he seldom fails in his judgement or skill. How many errands he handles on the stage road; parcels purchased and carried, from cambric needle to grindstone. And the treasure he carries, bills he pays, and how honestly. Bank presidents, brokers and men in high stations may embezzle, but not the Prince of the Ribbons. He is not overpaid for all this, but he had one consolation. There is none so high, none so rich, none so profane, none so religious, none so poorly dressed or richly clad, but they all want to sit alongside the driver.

"Presidents, priests, editors, judges, Senators, my ladies with the golden tresses and rich laces, all are troubled with the same weakness: 'Agent, give me a seat alongside the driver.'"

Article by one C. C. Bush, 9/5/1878
Courtesy of The El Dorado Historical Museum

TIPS FOR STAGECOACH TRAVELERS

The best seat inside a stage is the one next to the driver. Even if you have a tendency to sea-sickness when riding backwards... you'll get over it and will get less jolts and jostling. Don't let any "sly elph" trade you his mid-seat.

In cold weather don't ride with tight-fitting boots, shoes, or gloves. When the driver asks you to get off and walk do so without grumbling, he won't request it unless absolutely necessary. If the team runs away...sit still and take your chances. If you jump, nine out of ten times you will get hurt. In very cold weather abstain entirely from liquor when on the road, because you will freeze twice as quickly when under its influence.

Don't growl at the food received at the station...stage companies generally provide the best they can get.

Don't keep the stage waiting. Don't smoke a strong pipe inside the coach. Spit on the leeward side. If you have anything to drink in a bottle pass it around. Procure your stimulants before starting, as "ranch" (stage depot) whiskey is not "Nectar."

Don't lean or lop over neighbors when sleeping. Take small change to pay expenses. Never shoot on the road, as the noise might frighten the horses. Don't discuss politics or religion.

Don't point out where murders have been committed, especially if there are woman passengers.

Don't lag at the washbasin. Don't grease your hair, because travel is dusty. Don't imagine for a moment that you are going on a picnic. Expect annoyances, discomfort, and some hardships.

Omaha Herald, 1877
From the Historical Museum, Placerville
June, 1988

Courtesy of The California State Library

✦━━━━━━━━━━━━━━━━✦

Maude Hulbert Horn, editor and publisher of the
Georgetown Gazette at a time when there were less than 50 women
editors in the state of California.

Chapter 11

MAUDE HULBERT HORN

A 19th-Century Publisher

T he *Mountain Democrat* in Placerville called her The *Gazette's* "editress," and the *San Francisco Call* described her as "gifted editor, writer and manager." She was Maude Hulbert Horn, a reporter for the *Georgetown Gazette* at 14 and its publisher two years later at age 16.

Maude Hulbert Horn was born in 1875 and grew up with printer's ink in her veins. She was the daughter of Celia Welleford Hulbert and Joseph Hulbert, a publisher. In 1880 the family moved from Auburn, California, to Georgetown. Hulbert was impressed with the town's gold mining opportunities and the fact that it was a small bustling trade center with an air of permanence. The first *Georgetown Gazette* was published on April 9, 1880.

Once the newspaper was established, Hulbert started prospecting for gold, leaving the responsibility of the *Gazette* to his wife Celia. During the next few years, the family increased, and Maude, the oldest of four children, had to assume a great deal of the *Gazette's* duties. The other children were not interested in the paper.

At the age of nine, Maude was taught to set type with a steel-type stick that was cut to fit the child's small hand, and, by the time Maude was 14, she was recognized as a reporter. She attended public school where she excelled in English literature. In 1891, at 16, her father named Maude editor of the *Gazette*. Her name, however, did not appear on the masthead for two years, and then she was titled manager instead of editor. Maude had to give up her plans of attending college, along with social activities, to maintain the family weekly newspaper.

The young woman was running the paper by 1895, with help only on press day and whenever Hulbert returned from the mines. Her desire to learn continued, and Maude found the time to study French, Shakespeare, astronomy, and shorthand.

In 1896 her mother passed away, and Maude became responsible for her younger siblings. She took over management of the household as well as the *Gazette*. Her father still spent most of his time in the mines, and Maude, who had planned to become a court reporter in Sacramento, gave up her own career for the sake of the family.

The demands of the home were so great that the young woman, who weighed only 97 pounds, felt her name should be dropped from the paper. Later a woman was hired to help with the family, and Maude again began to run the newspaper. Her name was not returned to the masthead even though Hulbert had moved to Oregon leaving the *Gazette* in Maude's control.

John C. "Jack" Horn joined the *Gazette*, and two years later he and Maude were married. Horn was an experienced printer, and together their coverage gained the respect of Georgetown. It was Maude's policy not to print items that might cause embarrassment. Many times she would omit a birth notice so readers wouldn't know how long the woman had been married. When a local resident was involved in an indiscretion, it went unreported.

Although Maude was the legal owner and publisher of the *Gazette*, her husband was identified as the sole editor and proprietor of the paper. Maude's thoughts about the subject were not recorded; it appears she was used to taking a backstage role, as were many women of that period. Maude had placed herself second to her father and later to her husband when it came to recognition. Although Horn had the title, Maude held the responsibility as reporter, manager, and editor of the paper.

The Horns began to raise a family of their own, and following the birth of their children, Maude again had a household as well as a newspaper to look after.

Her oldest daughter Amy learned to set type and showed an interest in the family enterprise. At mealtime Maude, with a notebook beside her, would ask each child what he or she had seen that day and what was new. The children learned to spell the names correctly and provide accurate facts. They gathered news from events as carefully as their mother. Amy went to all the funerals with Maude and helped gather information for the *Gazette*. Because it was inappropriate to take notes at a funeral, Amy would walk slowly and watch out of the corners of her eyes to see if there were out-of-town guests and then count the pallbearers. She would write about it later.

Maude was also a joiner and belonged to many organizations. They provided news and allowed her to socialize. She preferred to serve as a secretary in these groups because her dues were automatically paid. She also belonged to many lodges.

Maude spent a considerable amount of time without her husband Jack. His brother's business had been destroyed by the San Francisco earthquake and fire in 1906. The Horns borrowed money to set them up in a new venture. Jack Horn took their daughter Amy and moved to San Francisco to help out. Maude tried to hire a printer for the paper, but found she could do it faster alone. She worked herself into exhaustion, and it was common for her to faint at moments of stress. The children grew up so accustomed to seeing their mother faint that they would just put her into a clothes basket, carry her to the nearest couch, and lay her down until she regained consciousness.

Money was scarce in the Horn household, and over the years both husband and wife had to move into part-time jobs. Jack sold insurance and became a photographer. Maude wrote, as a stringer, for *The Sacramento Bee* and submitted material to the *Mountain Democrat* in Placerville and the *Auburn Journal*. She also sold home-grown cherries. With her husband gone, Maude had to continue all the extra jobs alone.

Jack and Amy returned home after a two-year absence in San Francisco, and the Horns resumed their business ventures together. Maude became involved with community projects. During World War I, she directed Red Cross public health and relief efforts, and, following the war, she attended a League of Nations meeting as an honorary delegate.

In 1921, while taking care of business in Placerville, Jack Horn was killed trying to rescue a woman in a fire. Two weeks later Hulbert passed away, and Maude found herself alone. She kept the *Gazette* going in order to send her son to college. Upon his graduation, Maude merged the paper with the *Mountain Democrat*. She had spent over 40 years with the *Gazette* and wanted a less confining life. Public reaction to the merger was interesting...the *San Francisco Chronicle* ran a male-dominated history of the *Gazette* glorifying Horace Hulbert and Jack Horn. The final sentence read: "Since the death of her husband, Mrs. Maude Horn has been the publisher."

Maude sold all the *Gazette's* equipment and took a vacation in

Hawaii. Later she studied genealogy and was accepted into both the state and national societies of The Daughters of the American Revolution. She had prominent friends all over California and became one of the jurors in El Dorado County's first Superior Court trial. Three years later she was a part of the Grand Jury, and in 1930 Maude was appointed Justice of the Peace. She was the first woman in Georgetown to hold this position and served for three years.

Maude never stopped being a newspaperwoman. Toward the end of her life, when her daughter Amy once again started printing the *Gazette*, she wrote a regular column.

Maude Horn died in 1935. Public records of her newspaper were almost non-existent. She had been downplayed or ignored throughout her career. Few women of that era were recognized for their contributions...most were neglected in the historical accounts.

Records of Maude Horn and her many achievements can be found at the El Dorado Library and Chamber of Commerce as well as in Georgetown. She was a woman who was many things...wife, mother, reporter, editor, and publisher...at a time when there were less than 50 women editors in California. Her role in journalism will remain a part of that area's exciting past.

Maude Hulbert Horn and Jack Horn on their wedding day.

From the book, I Remember, courtesy of The El Dorado County Chamber of Commerce

◆―――――――――――――――――――――◆

The couple were married in Yuba City.
He was an experienced newspaper man who worked at the
San Francisco Chronicle by day and taught dancing at night.
She was the editor and manager of the Georgetown Gazette.
On July 31, 1898, their first child, a girl named Amy was born.
A boy, John Hulbert, and a girl Doris,
completed the Horn family.

From the book, I Remember, courtesy of The El Dorado Chamber of Commerce

◆——————————————————————◆

*Maude Hulbert Horn was recognized as a reporter at 14,
and in 1891, at the age of 16, her father
named her editor of The Georgetown Gazette.*

From the book, I Remember, courtesy of The El Dorado Chamber of Commerce

Jack Horn, Maude Hulbert's husband.
He left the San Francisco Chronicle to work for her at the
Georgetown Gazette.

GEORGETOW

H. W. Hulbert, Publisher. }
Established April 9. 1880. }

GEORGETOWN, EL DO

STAGE LINES.

TO AUBURN—Leave Georgetown 5:00 A. M.; Arrive at Auburn, 10 A M; Leave Auburn, 4 P.M. Arrive at Georgetown, 9 PM. (Sunday excepted)

TO PLACERVILLE—Leave Georgetown, Mondays, Wednesdays & Fridays, at 7 A. M.; Arrive in Georg town, Tuesdays, Thursdays and Saturdays, at P. M.

PROFESSIONAL.

WM. BURTON, A. M., C. E.

U. S. Deputy Surveyor, Notary Public, Civil Engineer.

P. O. Garden Valley, Cal.

G. F. DEETKEN,

Mining, Consulting and Civil Engineer

REPORTS UPON MINING PROPERTIES, surveys Mines, Railroads and Canals, and superintends the workings of same; assays of ores and mineral analysis attended to with special care.

ADDRESS ; Auburn, Placer Co. Cal.　　sc7

FOUNDRY AFD MACHINE SHOP

H. S. MOREY, PLACERVILLE, CAL. MANufacturer of Quartz, Saw and Grist Mills, And all kinds of iron and brass castings.

CHAS. F. IRWIN,

ATTORNEY-AT-TAW. OFFICE, OPposite Court House, Main St. Placerville.

E. L. CRAWFORD,

NOTARY PUBLIC AND INSURANCE Agent. Office, 71 Church St. Georgetown, California.

I. P. JACKSON,

NOTARY PUBLIC AND INSURANCE Agent for the Western Assurance, of Toronto, and the Imperial of London, Insurance Companies. Office, Georgetown, California.

F. R. J. DIXON,

NOTARY PUBLIC, REAL ESTATE AND Collection Office, GREENWOOD, Cal Applications for Mining and Agricultural Patents drawn and filed in the U. S. Land Office.

HUTCHINSON & MANN,

GENERAL INSURANCE AGENTS, 322 and 324 California Street, San Francisco. Greenwood Agency, F. R. J. DIXON.

MINING RECORDER

—Mr. and Mrs. Frank Forbes came down from the Rubicon Springs last week.

—E. L. Crawford has a large, vigorous chestnut tree in his orchard well loaded with nuts. The chestnut thrives in its greatest perfection here.

—Thos. E. Jones, who has been absent about seven years, arrived last Monday at the home of his parents in this place Mr. and Mrs. Samuel Jones. He came down from British Columbia.

—The Ferguson Ranch, just east of town, has a large amount of choice fruit, including apples, pears, plums and grapes, and we came near saying honey, for we received a sample of that sort of fruit from that ranch last week, which was delicious. Ferguson has slathers of fruit.

—Our neighbor E. C. Cheek is building himself a new residence on his lot adjoining the Gazette lot on the south. H. M. Dains, assisted by Jake Wolfe and A. W. Porter, are putting up the building. We are glad to know that neighbor Cheek is able to stem the storm, and hope he will pull safely through.

—Last Saturday we had the pleasure of an introduction to Andrew Ellicott and W. A. Root, who are down from the Rubicon, on their way to the wilds of Eastern Oregon, where they go by water by way of Portland, to meet John and Robt. Pridgeon, who started overland Sept. 2d. The company have gone up to engage in hunting and trapping this winter.

Our Democratic friends don't like the way the Republicans are kicking up such a racket in the East. They say it isn't fair for Mr. Blaine to go from city to city magnetising the people so —that he ought to stay at home like Mr. Cleveland does, and attend to his own business. Poor Grover ! He is a bully fellow at home among the boys, but he cant magnetize worth a cent out among the millions.

—The Rev. Father Goodwin of Chicago Ill., will deliver a lecture in the Catholic Church, Georgetown, on Sunday October 5th at 7 P. M. The subject will be "The Catholic Church and its work in the United States." The public are cordially and earnestly invited.

—Papaw. Many of our readers came from the land where this fruit grows in its native condition, and its very mention to many will bring fond remembrances of childhood's days. It has been demonstrated by Lewis Sites, a few miles west of Georgetown, that the papaw flourishes even better on the Georgetown Divide than in its native home. He has trees five years from the

The great manufacturers now is Know-N heaven, and ca culated to oper adopted citizer from the debris Nothing ghost, garments, the c exclaimed "E these Democra water,"

Ohio is s some majority Democratic ma without stint; managers have Democracy at t have started money," and su journals now su are becoming proaches—they

"Support factories," "enc Industries," me renumerative i publican party cause it encoun ployment for la It encourages t sources. All th energy with ca not protected, t the power of ca and strong. N times wields un Free Trade Aris its wealth by s nations and lan capital in Engla ed by men gage enterprises. O resources, is the can party is the Democratic part notional, envio leaders, the Bo bred and nurtu Bourbon Democ perate effort to They would stee er of which to d voters. Will th mit them to ele down to Superv

GAZETTE.

., CAL., OCT., 3 1884.   VOL. 5. NO. 27

me of the
a literature
e ransacked
al best cal-
ces of our
ught forth
the Know-
igh colored
in glee and
reward of
arrel of ice

by a hand-
where the
ng money
Republican
nmated the
re-formers"
orporation
Democratic
hio. They
e end ap-
ossible.

and Manu-
of Home
It means
The Re-
labor, be-
reates em-
Progress.
r vast re-
dominable
capital is
ted. It is
ions great
ital some-
denced in
sh obtains
ing other
a, unlike
d control-
internal
sh it vast
Republi-
while the
cranky—
aat is its
stly men
d. These
and des-
s Fall.—
nder cov-
uspecting
unty per-
Senator
fever !

WE desire to call the attention of our Democratic readers who are inclined to favor Free Trade doctrine to the following:

"In the forty-second annual report of the Registrar General (page 27) we find that of the total number of deaths in 1879, one out of every fifteen died in a work-house; while in London, the wealthiest city in the world, one out of nine died in the work-house.—Among the 600,000 out-door paupers there are, doubtless, more deaths than among the 190,000 in-door paupers. If this be so, one out of about every seven of our population end their days as paupers."

Just think of this friends, in England after more than fifty years of Free Trade, one in seven of the population end their days as paupers. The above quotation is from the official record of the British government.

A passage in Blaine's Rochester speech should be impressed upon the mind of every voter. The Plumed Knight thus concisely stated the platform of the Republican party:

The Republican party embodies in its creed four distinct and important doctrines: First, peace with the whole world; Second, commercial expansion in every practicable direction; Third, the encouragement of every form of American industry; Fourth, protection of every citizen, native or naturalized, at home or abroad.

These are living issues. Greatest of them all is the protection and encouragement of every form of American industry. And what do the Democrats oppose to it? Competition with every American industry, under free trade with all foreign countries. Voters can take their choice.

WHEREVER Blaine has shown himself of late, the most unbounded en-

—It is gratifying to state that Mr. Epps is improving nicely. Remember he is a candidate for Constable.

There are in Ohio five German daily papers—three in Cincinnati, one in Cleveland, and one in Toledo. All of them are zealously supporting BLAINE & LOGAN.

New York Star (Dem.): Should Cleveland be defeated in November, it is safe to predict a breaking up of the Solid South and a reconstruction of the Democratic party.

Well informed readers can readily see that the ends and aims of the Democratic writers is to deceive those who have the misfortune not to be well informed in the political history of the country.

THE sand-lot or anti-enterprise element of the Democracy, delight setting on their haunches, and calling themselves "reformers."

FOR CONSTABLE.

T. B. EPPS is a candidate for Constable for Georgetown Township.

FOR CONSTABLE.

. W. PORTER is a candidate for Constable for Georgetown Township.

FOR CONSTABLE.

WM. PARKHURST is a candidate for Constable for Georgetown Township.

THE Republican favors the election of Geo. H. Ingham for Superior Judge and gives some very good reasons why Republicans should support his

IN accepting Grover Cleveland, the Examiner has been forced to eat crow. The Republican papers are now publishing an editorial from the Examiner of March 12, 1883, entitled "Governor Cleveland's Course," which is

Courtesy of The California State Library

Courtesy of The Nevada Historical Society

◆——————————————————————◆

This photo is said to be of Eilley Orrum in her early years.
Although the photograph was obtained from the
Nevada Historical Society, they do not guarantee its authenticity.
Many Historian's, however, believe this is a true picture of Eilley.

Chapter 12

EILLEY ORRUM

◆ ―――――――――――――――――――――――――――――――――――― ◆
The Lady of the Mansion

A s a young girl, Allison "Eilley" Orrum realized she was destined for a life of success and riches. She knew it as she ran over the grassy moors and climbed the craggy ridges of her homeland in the Highlands of Scotland. She saw her future etched in the clouds and read it in the stars that filled the evening sky. Eilley had a rare gift: with the help of a glass sphere she called a peep-stone, she could see the future.

Eilley, however, saw only a part of the things to come. Her famous crystal ball showed a vast fortune and a mansion. It did not reveal the personal grief she would suffer.

Eilley Orrum was born in Scotland in 1826. She was a high-spirited young woman who was filled with ambition and a burning desire to achieve fame and fortune. Unfortunately, Scotland, in the 1800s had little to offer, so Eilley, in order to escape, converted to Mormonism. She gave up the traditional Presbyterian faith of her homeland, and, with several hundred converts, she sailed for America. The large group arrived in the United States in 1843 and traveled on to the Mormon colony at Nauvoo, Illinois.

Although Eilley had eagerly anticipated Nauvoo, her first impressions were less than ecstatic. Instead of grandeur, she found unpaved dusty streets, a half-completed community, and a shortage of eligible men. However, the undaunted, red-haired, buxom Eilley managed to find a husband despite the lack of bachelors. She married the Elder Hunter, a prime mover in the Mormon church who was old enough to be her father. It has been said he married her because he needed someone to help work his farm and wanted children in his later years. Eilley married him to enjoy the prestige of being "The Elder's" wife. The couple followed Brigham Young to Salt Lake City, and Eilley did not produce any children. Their marriage ended when the Elder decided to practice polygamy.

Eilley secured a divorce and found employment at a trading store. While working there, a customer offered to sell a sphere of glass the size of a duck egg that he said was a crystal ball. Eilley immediately recognized the sphere as a peep-stone, similar to the one she had used in Scotland to help her see into the future. Eilley bought the crystal. She had to work one day without wages to pay for it, and the stone became the window to Eilley's life.

One day, while peering into her mystical stone, Eilley saw a vision of a green valley with a blue lake surrounded by large mountains. She knew that this was the special place where her fame and fortune would be found. Realizing she couldn't find the valley alone, the practical Eilley married Alex Cowan, a gentle Mormon who farmed the land and had never been wed. In 1854 they joined a group of Latter-Day Saints who were moving West to establish a new colony in the Carson Valley. Eilley was filled with excitement...surely this would be the place in her crystal ball.

However, instead of a sparkling lake, they found a sluggish creek and barren mountainous land. Disappointed, Eilley urged her easy-going husband to move on, and several days later they found her valley. It was as it appeared in the peep-stone, large and grassy, with a beautiful lake. Eilley took a deep breath and looked out over the landscape. In her mind she saw a mansion with many rooms, gardens, and flowing fountains. She also saw happy children. The couple carefully marked off the half-section of land and together Eilley and Alex built a cabin. The only thing missing was money and Alex's ambition to earn it.

Before winter set in, Eilley and Alex left their homestead and moved to Gold Hill, a new town that had started to grow. Eilley, gazing into her peep-stone, saw pieces of gold, miners, and wagons. She felt there was money to be made in the new community of tents and saloons, and she was determined to have her share. Alex built a cabin, and Eilley started taking in boarders. Their joint venture was successful until her husband received a message from Brigham Young to return to Salt Lake City. Alex Cowan, who was always a strong Mormon, left immediately taking their wagons and livestock. Eilley stayed behind, alone in a lawless town with only her peep-stone and herself to depend upon. She was 32 years old...and childless.

The Scots are noted for being frugal and hard-working, and Eilley was no exception. She started taking in laundry as well as boarders. Her rule was that she would cook, wash, and care for the miners—but her bed was hers alone. Eilley was motherly and took care of the men's needs through domesticity. Her meals were wholesome and substantial. She served no alcohol in her establishment, and women were not allowed. When the laundry chores became too difficult, due to the hard water of the area, Eilley bought a little donkey cart and started taking the clothes to Washoe Valley's hot springs to wash. There she scrubbed and mended for the miners. She also divorced her second husband, Alex Cowan, for desertion. Her peep-stone developed a new vision: it displayed streaks of black sand.

The boarding house flourished, but Eilley was not getting rich. One of the miners offered her his claim for an unpaid bill and Eilley accepted. The claim beside it belonged to Lemuel Sanford "Sandy" Bowers, a young teamster who had recently arrived in Gold Hill. He also boarded with Eilley. One evening, following a party, Sandy asked Eilley to share her life with him as well as her claim. She agreed, and the happy couple left for a honeymoon. The groom, 26, was eight years younger than the bride.

When the Bowers returned to Gold Hill, they were wealthy. The black streaks of sand Eilley had seen in the peep-stone were silver, and, together their claims made them two of the richest millionaires in Gold Hill. Sandy had no problem spending the money...the ambitious Eilley took care of that. She built a mansion on the site of her old homestead in the Washoe Valley. Special stonecutters came from Scotland to fit the blocks of granite together. Eilley wanted to furnish the inside of the mansion with opulence. She and Sandy decided to go on a spending spree to find furnishings "finer than anyone in the Comstock had seen." Sandy declared "Money ain't no object!" And the couple, one illiterate and the other with illusions of grandeur, left for a European shopping tour. They were extravagant and paid at least twice as much as everything was worth. Eilley purchased marble in Italy, carpets with special designs, and heavy ornate furniture including a chair that resembled a throne.

The Bowers wore only the finest silks and brocades. Eilley had a special dress made of royal purple, with a pattern of roses stitched in pure gold at the hem and lace at the throat and wrists. She was determined to visit Queen Victoria. The queen, however, did not receive divorced women, and a woman who had been divorced twice was totally unacceptable. Disappointed, Eilley and her husband left for home. They took a few cuttings from Westminster Abby to plant at their mansion and sailed for America aboard The Persia, a luxury liner.

While on their return trip, the mother of a new infant died and was buried at sea. Eilley, who reputedly had lost two children she had born while married to Sandy, adopted the child. They named her Margaret after Eilley's mother and Persia for the ship. At this point the Bowers' history is not quite clear. There are no records of the birth of Eilley's two children or of their deaths. Sandy, in his will, named Persia as the only product of his marriage, and there are three graves behind the mansion: Sandy's, Persia's, and Eilley's. It is possible that Persia was the only child of their union and that she was not adopted as the books say. It is also possible that there were no other children.

When the Bowers returned home, Sandy felt he had been neglecting the mine, so he moved to Gold Hill. Eilley spent her time caring for the mansion. It was the happiest period of her life; surely all her dreams and visions had been fulfilled. She had the mansion, a child and Sandy. The peep-stone was put away, and Persia's playmates filled the house; Eilley's love of children grew and expanded.

Her happiness, however, was not meant to last. In 1868 Eilley's world fell apart. She was called to Sandy's bedside in Gold Hill, and a few hours after she arrived he died of Silicosis, or miner's disease. Eilley had an elaborate funeral and brought Sandy home. He was buried on the hill above the mansion, and Eilley was a widow.

The silver of the Comstock gave out in 1867, and the business deals in which Sandy had been involved were poorly handled. Creditors started arriving at the door of the mansion, and everything Eilley owned had either been mortgaged or badly invested by Sandy. She tried borrowing the money, and when that failed, she attempted to support Persia and herself by turning the mansion into a hotel. While expanding the mansion, Eilley sent Persia to Reno to board with friends. Soon afterwards, Eilley received a call from her friends that Persia was ill; before she arrived, the child died. Her body was brought home and buried beside Sandy's. All of Eilley's plans had gone awry, and in 1875 she lost the mansion by default. The ornate furnishings were auctioned off.

Eilley was penniless. She started telling fortunes, with the aid of her crystal ball and became known as the "Washoe Seeress." Eventually the visions in her peep-stone vanished, and in 1903, at age 77, Eilley Orrum Bowers died. She was brought home to rest and today lies at peace next to Sandy and Persia. Their graves, on a tree-studded hill, overlook the mansion Eilley dreamed of as a child as well as the beautiful valley she saw in her famous peep-stone.

BOWERS MANSION

Half-way between Reno and Carson City, in the Washoe Valley, one of the most impressive restored historical homes in the state of Nevada can be found.

The two-story granite stone mansion of 16 rooms was built with the fortune that L. S. "Sandy" Bowers and his psychic wife, Eilley Orrum, earned from their mine in Gold Hill, Nevada. Many acknowledge this couple to be Nevada's first Comstock Lode millionaires, acquiring their wealth between 1859-1867. The mansion was completed by 1864, and generally accepted to have cost $200,000 to build and furnish.

The Bowers Mansion and 46 acres of land were purchased by Washoe County in 1966, providing the final restoration of the mansion, and returning it to the original two-story structure. All the rooms are elegantly appointed with Victorian antiques.

Original furnishings from earlier days tell the story of the millionaires who built the structure and were the proud owners for 11 years. A rosewood piano dominates one corner of the library, along with many of the original 1,000 volumes that once filled the bookcases. There are ornate marble fireplaces imported from Italy, gold mirrors, and carpets decorated with roses. On a table in the parlor there is a daguerreotype of Eilley Bowers taken in the late 1870s. The photograph is called a "Spirit Picture" because of the shadowy figure of a child looking over Eilley's shoulder. Since there were no trick photographers in the 1800s, many people believe it is the ghost of her daughter, Persia. A crystal ball sits beside the picture.

The mansion went through a series of owners. Eventually the building became dilapidated, with broken windows and doors falling apart. It remained alone and isolated, surrounded by grass and grazing cattle, until 1946 when the Reno Women's Civic Club initiated the original purchase. Later, Washoe County contributed the balance, and many of the original furnishings were donated back by local citizens.

Today, happy families picnic on the grass, while laughing children splash in the large swimming pool fed by natural hot springs. The mansion has been restored to its former splendor and informative tours are available between Memorial Day and Labor Day.

Courtesy of The Nevada Historical Society

◆ ━━━━━━━━━━━━━━━━━━━━━━━━ ◆

Mrs. Bowers

Courtesy of The Nevada Historical Society

Sandy Bowers

Courtesy of The Nevada Historical Society

Margaret Persia Bowers.
Beloved daughter of Sandy and Eilley Bowers.
Died at the age of 12 years old in July, 1874.

BOWERS MANSION

Dedicated in Honor of The Sons and Daughters
of Nevada, Veterans of World War II.

Erected by Sandy Bowers and his wife, Eilley Orrum, in 1864.
With the Gold and Silver from their mine on the Comstock.

Purchased in 1946 by Popular Subscription and Washoe County
as a playground for the children of the State.

Courtesy of Joe and Beverly Cola

◆─────────────────────◆

Sarah Fossati and her mother Candida Lombardo.
Sarah, the co-owner of Smith's Flat House, spoke five languages
and was an excellent innkeeper and cook.

Chapter 13

SARAH FOSSATI
19th-Century Businesswoman

T he mile houses along Highway 50 from Placerville to Virginia City were important stopping places for miners, teamsters, and freight carriers on their way to the Comstock Lode. They were run with varying degrees of success; one of the best of them was Smith's Flat House, managed by Sarah Fossati, a woman who spoke five languages, and was an excellent innkeeper and cook.

During the 1860s, traffic on the highway was so heavy that any driver who dropped out would have to wait until the procession stopped for the night to get back in line. If he became impatient and attempted to pass the line, the vehicle was likely to roll off the shoulder into the deep canyon below.

Although traffic had slowed by the 1880s, when Sarah Lombardo became the wife of Smith's Flat House owner Nicola Fossati, it was still a busy place. The large establishment boasted of a boarding house and saloon and had many outbuildings...all of which the young bride was expected to help manage.

Sarah Fossati was born in El Dorado County in 1866. She was the daughter of "John" Napoleon Lombardo from Genoa, Italy, and Candida Quanchi of Maggia, Switzerland. Napoleon met Candida after he moved from Italy to Smith's Flat. Candida traveled alone from Switzerland over the Isthmus of Panama to San Francisco, and came to El Dorado County to live with relatives. The couple met at a social function and were soon wed. They homesteaded about two miles from Smith's Flat, building a home from the natural stones in the area. Later it was called The Old Stone House. Sarah was ten years old when they built the house and helped by carrying stones.

The family farmed the land growing vegetables and fruits, and later opened a small winery to produce sacramental wine for the Catholic church. Today the winery is called the Boeger Winery, and the basement of the old house is used for a tasting room. Sarah learned at an early age to help with the farm and work in the winery.

When Sarah started school at age six, she was a fast-learning student who excelled at her studies. Upon completion of the third grade, her mother decided Sarah didn't need any further education. It seemed Candida felt girls should spend their time helping at home. Her father Napoleon had a different opinion, however, because he continued to tutor Sarah. He was the son of a career officer, who had served under Napoleon III in the Crimean War, and at one time he had a private tutor. Napoleon was well-educated, and under his guidance, Sarah learned to speak French, Italian, Spanish and excellent English. Later she gained a workable knowledge of Chinese. All of this helped her when she became a part of Smith's Flat House. She was considered very learned for a girl of that era.

Sarah's mother was a stern person, who was strict and of the opinion that children should obey and not ask questions. Because of this, the young girl and her father developed a close relationship, and she accompanied him on many business trips. While on one of these trips, Sarah met Nicola Fossati, a gentleman from Italy. She was 18 years old and Nicola, who had just become the sole owner of Smith's Flat House, decided to marry the healthy girl. He was 11 years older than Sarah, and, following a proper courtship, they were married in 1885.

Marriage for Sarah added many responsibilities to her life. She was expected to take over management of Smith's Flat House, including doing all the work. It had two floors; on the first was the general store, saloon, card room, post office, and living quarters for the family. Upstairs there were 11 rooms for boarders and a large dance hall that was used as a community center for political meetings, precinct voting, dancing, traveling shows, and auditorium for other large gatherings. At first Sarah was overwhelmed; however, she soon adjusted to supervising the business.

She prepared fine dinners for the family, guests, and boarders. Her old wood cookstove had a warming oven where she would keep the food hot. Watching Sarah select wood from the woodbox in the corner of the kitchen was fascinating. She had learned which type of wood was best for whatever she was about to prepare and would pick and sort carefully. Her food was excellent, as well as thrifty. She raised all the vegetables, cultivating them with an Italian Soppa, which is a rake with two tines, 12-inches long. She usually had one woman helper.

Later when her children were older, Sarah kept a beautiful flower garden and was especially proud of her lovely roses.

Since Sarah was also expected to manage the post office and general store, she needed to learn bookkeeping. The agent for Sperry Flour offered to teach her and was amazed at how fast the young woman learned. Within a few weeks, Sarah could accurately keep the books and ledgers for Smith's Flat House.

When a young arrival from Italy, John Lagomarsino, needed help learning English and arithmetic, it was natural that Sarah would become his tutor. She was obviously quite successful. Later the young man was instrumental in helping A. P. Giannini found the Bank of Italy, now known as the Bank of America. The Fossati records also show that this same enterprising young man was the grandfather of United States Congressman Robert Lagomarsino of Santa Barbara County, California.

Sarah was a sturdy woman who was self-conscious of her large feet. She wore long dresses with high collars, full sleeves, and set-in belts. She pulled her thick black hair back into a bun at the nape of her neck. Sarah was neat in her appearance as well as her books, ledgers, and home. She was a shy person and always kept a low profile. When asked to join the Native Daughters of California as a charter member, she declined, preferring to live a quiet life with her husband and children.

Whenever there was a question that needed to be answered, however, people would come to Sarah. Her memory was excellent, and she could recall an event from years back better than the record books. She was also sought after for advice and interesting stories. Everyone enjoyed her little touches of humor.

Besides supervising Smith's Flat House, Sarah also added improvements to the hotel. One of her most important contributions was a roof that extended across the road so the ladies could alight from their carriages without getting wet during inclement weather. Many of the women, who wore fancy gowns, had Sarah to thank for her thoughtfulness.

While Sarah kept the ledgers and supervised the hotel and store, Nicola maintained the corrals and took care of the stock. He was fond of fast horses, and if he could have driven a car like he rode a horse, he would have been a race driver today. He was continuously improving the land around Smith's Flat House. One of his innovations was to use the rocks left from the early mining days to build a series of terraces to catch the silt from the mountains above. These plots formed pastures for the horses and were used to grow hay for the cows.

In his late 50s, Nicola started having problems with his legs and could not perform the heavy labor as before, so he took over as a genial host and would entertain the many guests.

There were two things Sarah was firm about during her lifetime. She would not take care of the saloon or card room. "Nic" supervised them. The gaming tables were covered to keep the noise down, and Sarah had a good reason for disliking the saloon. One of her babies became ill, and when the doctor arrived, he stopped at the saloon on the way to care for the infant. When he finally saw the child, the doctor was so drunk he didn't know what he was doing; the baby died. The other thing Sarah insisted upon was attending church as often as possible, especially on holy days.

Nicola Fossati died in 1925. Sarah's health began to fail in 1947, and she died at the age of 81. During Sarah's lifetime, it is doubtful that she ever left Smith's Flat (later known as Smithflat), except for an occasional visit to Placerville. Yet she managed to reach out and touch the lives of many, including a young man from Italy. Although Sarah Fossati will never be famous, she lives in memories and records of the Fossati family of Smith's Flat.

1923. From: Bankitaly Life. September 1923.
Lagomarsino, John.   Vol. 7. #9. p. 13.

In the death of our respected vice-president, John Lagomarsino of Ventura, on September 27, our bank lost an officer who had a very strong hold on the affections of his co-workers throughout our entire banking system.

His demise followed an automobile accident in Lompoc, and when the end came all the members of his family were at his bedside.

The funeral took place in Ventura, from the Old Mission Church, and was attended by mourners from all over California, who came to pay their last tribute of love to one of Ventura's foremost citizens. Every store, bank and public office was closed during the funeral.

Mr. Lagomarsino was born in Genoa 59 years ago, and had been a resident of Ventura for thirty-eight years. At the time of his passing he was fostering some great horticultural enterprises, besides being actively interested in the Bank of Italy, of which he was a vice-president and director.

John had a smile for everyone and always responded generously to appeals for help. Having risen from the "ranks." he knew something of privation and was therefore quick to answer a call of distress . . . .

Courtesy of The Bank of America Archives

From the book, I Remember, courtesy of The El Dorado Chamber of Commerce

◆————————————————————◆

Nicola Fossati and his sister, Mrs. Bessema.

THE LOMBARDO HOME

Courtesy of F. N. Fossati

*From the left standing in the foreground are
John Napolean Lombardo,
Sarah Fossati holding her son John, and Candida Lombardo.
Nicola Fossati is driving the team of black horses.
The stone house was built in 1876, and today the
basement is a tasting room for the Boeger Winery.*

ALL NIGHT
BALL AND SUPPER

• • • • • • • • • • • • • • •

AT NIC FOSSATI'S
SMITH'S FLAT

..Monday Eve, April 19, '97

TICKETS,   (Including Supper) $1.00

—◦◄ There will be a ►◦—

GRAND ✶ BALL.

Given at

Smith's Flat, on Friday Eve., Oct. 27, 1893.

A Fine Orchestra Has Been Secured   Good Time Assured.

TICKETS, Including Supper, - - - - **$1.50**

Courtesy of Joe and Beverly Cola

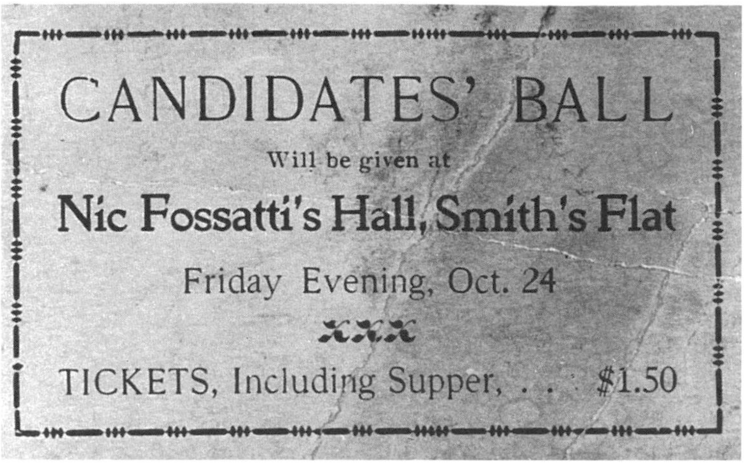

CANDIDATES' BALL

Will be given at

Nic Fossatti's Hall, Smith's Flat

Friday Evening, Oct. 24

xxx

TICKETS, Including Supper, . . . $1.50

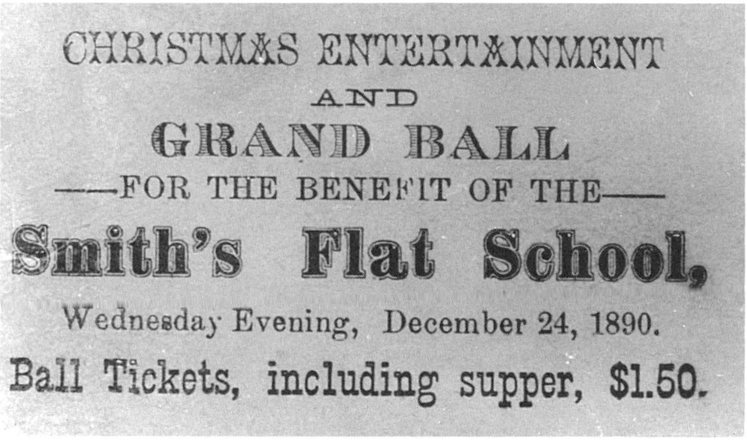

CHRISTMAS ENTERTAINMENT
AND
GRAND BALL
——FOR THE BENEFIT OF THE——
Smith's Flat School,

Wednesday Evening, December 24, 1890.

Ball Tickets, including supper, $1.50.

Courtesy of Joe and Beverly Cola

Courtesy of F. N. Fossati

A party at Smith's Flat House in 1895.
Seated center; Sarah and Nicola Fossati with their daughter Angie.

Drawing by Robin Isely

Eleanora

Chapter 14

ELEANORA DUMONT
A Gambling Lady

G ambling was an integral part of the early West. Cards were smoothly dealt by frozen-faced men behind the green-topped tables. It was a man's world where women were not allowed.

In 1854, however, this comfortable male-dominated profession was interrupted by a pretty young woman. She opened a gaming establishment, and with quick, nimble fingers started shuffling the deck. Her name was Eleanora Dumont; she was a gambling lady.

Eleanora Dumont arrived in Nevada City from San Francisco on a sweltering summer day in 1854. The lone woman passenger stepped down from the Sacramento stage, thanked the driver for a safe journey, and politely pointed out her expensive luggage. Then, with quiet dignity, she entered the hostelry.

Male onlookers whispered among themselves as they admired her trim figure, fresh young beauty, and the jaunty way she wore her flowered hat. The stylish woman went up to the desk and jotted her name: Madame Eleanora Dumont of New Orleans. Her past, like most of the people's in the West, was nobody's business.

For several weeks, Eleanora's presence generated speculation among the community. It was evident that the lady was of French heritage, but what was the sophisticated new arrival doing in Nevada City? Madame finally provided the answer when she calmly opened a public gambling saloon and expertly started dealing cards.

Eleanora named the establishment "Vingt-et-Un," which means "twenty-one." It was tastefully furnished with carpets and gas chandeliers. She served champagne instead of "Red Eye," and expected the clientele to be clean and groomed. The house was open 24 hours, and Madame paid all losses with a smile, while she quietly raked in the profits. No rowdies or women were allowed to enter the premises.

It was a novelty to see a beautiful young woman sitting at a gaming table shuffling cards. The miners poured in nightly to spend their precious metal. She commanded admiration and respect, and although her life was unusual, she gave no one a reason to question her chastity. It would seem that Madame Dumont had the ability to mine gold without digging for it, and the slight growth of fuzz that she had on her upper lip made her even more interesting.

Her success and beauty attracted many young men, none of whom interested the gambling lady. Eleanora's life became a constant struggle to fend off the male population. All her problems were solved when David Tobin, a professional gambler from New York, arrived and became her partner. Together they opened a larger establishment, adding poker, keno, and a faro-bank. Madame continued to deal twenty-one, remaining aloof from any sexual attachments.

Their partnership lasted for one prosperous year. In 1856 Tobin returned to New York, and Eleanora took her winnings to the rich mining community of Columbia. She set up her table in a hotel and continued her career. Gold was abundant, and many miners claimed they would rather lose their money to Madame than to win with someone else. Once more the profits flowed her way, and as she dealt, Eleanora began to stroke the fuzzy growth of hair on her upper lip.

The discovery of silver in 1859 created so much excitement that Eleanora decided to leave Columbia in search of more wealth in the Comstock. There are no records of her presence in Virginia City. She continued to travel, wandering from camp to camp, and she was always a favorite gambler. Madame Dumont was reputed to have been honest, generous to the losers, and many times provided the miners with a "stake." So great was her influence and charm over her rough associates that while dealing cards in Pioche, a rough town in southeastern Nevada, she settled a near riot with a laugh.

Eleanora lived a fast, hard life and realized that some day her luck would run out. She was not as young or beautiful as before, so she retired from her profession to buy a cattle ranch near Carson City, fulfilling a dream of many years. Raising cattle, however, wasn't easy for a gambling lady who knew very little about animal husbandry and even less about the land. The venture was filled with problems that she worked hard to overcome.

By the time the ranch began to show a profit, Eleanora felt tired and empty. She missed the thrills and excitement of her former life. The rewards of the ranch could not erase the sight of endless sagebrush, and she found little comfort in the lonely howl of coyotes.

When Jack McKnight, a cattle-buyer, entered her life, it was either lack of companionship or fate that made Eleanora marry him. McKnight was a worthless, small-time promoter who spent his time gambling at other people's expense. His interest in Eleanora was strictly for her money and ranch, not herself. She fell in love with his fancy clothing, fast-talking, and good looks. In one brief moment, all of her past experiences with men were forgotten. It didn't take long for her new husband to convince Eleanora to turn her money and property over to him. McKnight ran up debts, sold her ranch, and one day disappeared, leaving Eleanora penniless.

Eleanora returned to the mining towns and attempted to resume her career as a gambling lady. However, the shock of McKnight's desertion was so devastating that what was left of her beauty faded overnight. The abnormal growth on her upper lip became dark and coarse, and she soon acquired the name of "Madame Moustache."

Once more Madame wandered the mining camps of the Sierra, but her skill with the cards, too, was gone. She became an object of pity, and, in desperation, Eleanora put her cards away and moved to Bodie. There her dark moustache, along with stories of her past, made Madame a popular woman...and prostitute. She entered her new profession without enthusiasm; it was merely a way to survive. Men were fascinated by the hair upon her upper lip, and Eleanora started using alcohol to help her endure the life she was forced to live. The days of Madame Eleanora Dumont were gone; she had become the notorious Madame Moustache.

Gamblers and bartenders who had known her in better times befriended the unfortunate lady, but they could not give Eleanora back her charm and talent. One night, after a few drinks in a local saloon, she walked away and was never seen alive again. On September 8, 1897, her dead body was found about a mile out of town. Beside it lay a bottle of poison...Madame Eleanora Dumont had found her escape in suicide.

Thompson and West, noted historians, in their publication *History of Nevada County*, said: "Let her many good qualities invoke leniency in criticizing her failings." Eleanora's friends and the townspeople raised enough money to place her in consecrated ground. They made sure she had a permanent home...Madame was not buried in the outcasts' cemetery.

Courtesy of The Nevada Historical Society

◆⎯⎯⎯⎯⎯⎯⎯⎯◆

*Julia Bulette, the famous "Lady of the Red Light District."
She was a member of the "fair but frail" sisterhood,
and a prototype of all the fancy women in the early west.*

Chapter 15

JULIA BULETTE
◆ Lady of the Red Light District ◆

More has been written about Julia Bulette, both fact and fiction, then any other woman of the Comstock era. She was a member of the "fair but frail" sisterhood and a prototype of all the fancy women in the Early West.

While other women of easy virtue drifted into obscurity, Julia was destined to remain a part of Virginia City's colorful history. It may be that Julia became a legend because of her brutal murder, not for her many generous deeds.

Virginia City sprang up in 1859 following the discovery of the fabulous Comstock Lode. It became an overnight boomtown, with the busiest saloons in the mining area. The inhabitants, mostly men under 20 years of age, were robust and free-living. There were very few women, single or married.

At the center was C Street which consisted of businesses, saloons, and hotels. On the streets above C Street, the newly-made million-aires and elite lived in fine homes. Most of the unmarried miners, the prostitutes, and assorted working men lived below on D Street. The majority of the "ladies" could be found on the west side of D Street, in a five block area known as "The Red Light District"...possibly the first use of the now-famous description. The women were required to keep red-colored oil lamps hanging in their front windows. Further down the hill were the Chinese with their joss-houses, opium dens, and streets so narrow a coach could barely pass through. At the bottom of the hill, the Paiute and Washoe Indians made their camps.

There is very little documented history on Julia Bulette. She arrived in Virginia City about 1863 and was reputed to have been Creole from Louisiana. The Nevada Historical Society claims Julia was born in London or Liverpool, England, in 1832. She emigrated, with her family, to Louisiana when she was a child. Julia married early in life; however, the marriage was unsuccessful, and when it ended in divorce, she became a prostitute in New Orleans. The lure of gold drew Julia to California where she first worked the mining camps. She settled for a brief period in Weaverville before moving on to the Comstock.

Julia's cottage, or "crib," was located at a prime spot on the corner of Union and D Streets where the miners and workmen passed daily. It consisted of a parlor and bedroom. The parlor could accommodate as many as a dozen visitors and had lace curtains at the windows, a Brussels carpet, comfortable furniture, and cheery stove. Her bedroom was dominated by a large bed and was darkened by heavy curtains. It also had a trunk for her clothing, a wash-basin, and a spittoon. None of the other girls on the "row" had such elaborate furnishings. The cottages did not have indoor plumbing or kitchens.

Stories of Julia's wealth are highly exaggerated. It has been said she was the proprietress of an opulent establishment on C Street called "Julia's Palace," where she served French Champagne and gourmet food. However, there is no record of the business. Julia Bulette was merely a prostitute who lived on D Street and had more class than the rest. She was exceptionally kind-hearted and had many friends on the "row," but none worked for her. There is no validity in the stories that she had a fancy carriage pulled by a pair of matched Bays. The news media of that period would have written about any vehicle as elegant as her carriage was said to have been. It is hard to separate fact from myth when discussing Julia Bulette.

She was an attractive woman and considered a "good-sport." Very little is known about her personal life. She did know many men intimately and was considered a middle-class prostitute. Julia lived alone in her cottage, and like the rest of the "girls," made no plans for her future. She usually saw but one customer a night and did not have to solicit. Men sought her out. Julia chose who she pleased and often received as much as $1,000 a night for her services. Many of her clients were wealthy and appreciated her charms to the extent that they gave her expensive jewelry and furs. A good part of her earnings were spent on clothing, fancy lingerie (which could have been considered a business expense), and parties. Julia loved to entertain. Fresh flowers were delivered daily to her cottage via Wells Fargo, which on D Street was rare.

It can be assumed Julia dressed like the rest of the "ladies" of her class, wearing only the most fashionable gowns. The women liked bright-colored clothing, high-buttoned shoes, expensive furs, and jewelry. They were powdered or painted at a time when women did not wear makeup. The prostitutes usually paraded the streets in pairs and were called "street-walkers." However, the picture of Julia Bulette from the Nevada Historical Society is one of a dignified, almost severe woman.

Julia always had a friendly word for the workers who passed her cottage. Her many kind acts for the hard-working miners and donations to charity earned her a measure of respect and gratitude. She was never too busy to sit by the side of an injured or ill man and help nurse him back to health. Julia cared about them at a time when they had no one else.

One of the proudest moments in her career was the day she was made an honorary member of The Virginia Engine Company Number 1. Julia took her membership seriously. At the sound of the bell, she would rush to the fire along with the men and help man the pumps. She also gave money regularly for new equipment.

The day before Julia Bulette was murdered, in January 1867, was like any other in her life. She slept late, visited her friends, and went to see a performance at the opera house. Women of her class were required to sit in one of the boxes with the curtains drawn so they could see the entertainment and not be seen by the proper ladies. Julia was denied admission because she refused to sit in the section reserved for the "red-light women." She returned to her cottage early to wait for an appointment with a client.

The next day her body was found lying on her left side with her feet halfway out of the bed. Sometime during the night of January 20, 1867, she was strangled, shot, suffocated, and severely beaten. Her trunk with all her jewelry, furs, and personal possessions was stolen. Julia was only 35 years old.

The press called her murder "outrageous and cruel." The men and women she had befriended mourned her death and sought revenge for the brutal slaying. Julia's funeral was one of the largest and most expensive Virginia City had ever seen; even the saloons were closed. The fire department took up a collection and purchased an ornate, silver-handled casket. Julia, although a prostitute, had earned the respect and love of many. She was given a Catholic funeral. A large procession followed the casket which was led by the Metropolitan Brass Band. The Virginia Engine Company Number 1, in full uniform, wearing badges of mourning for their deceased member and benefactor, came next. Women of the "Red-Light District" wearing black and the men in their Sunday-best were last.

Julia was buried in a lonely grave about a mile east of town. A woman of easy virtue could not be buried in consecrated ground. They placed a large wooden marker over her grave with "JULIA" painted on it, and the mourners paid their last respects. On the return trip to Virginia City, the firemen sang "The Girl I Left Behind." The town was draped in black, and the respectable women hid behind shuttered windows, upset by the sight of their own husbands in the procession.

Several months later, John Millian, a French drifter, was arrested for the murder of Julia Bulette. They found her jewelry and furs in his possession. Millian claimed he wasn't guilty but knew the crime was going to happen. He said he was just keeping the property until the real murderer came to pick up Julia's things. It was very difficult to select a jury because of the hatred the town felt for Millian. However, he was eventually found guilty and condemned to die by hanging.

Many people felt the trial was unfair. The defense concluded that the prosecution had proved only one point...Julia Bulette was dead. Millian was a 35-year-old mild, inoffensive man, who seemed confused by the whole thing. The ladies of Virginia City felt sorry for the prisoner and brought him cakes and pies. They were always jealous of Julia, and unsuccessfully petitioned the Governor to commute Millian's sentence to life in prison.

At dawn on April 27, 1868, John Millian was hung. Excited people came by stage, horseback, or on foot from all the nearby towns, and the saloons closed for the second time. It became a spectator event, with everyone hoping to catch a glimpse of the murderer. Forty deputies and the National Guard in full uniform escorted the carriage carrying Millian and Father Manogue, priest of St. Mary's Catholic Church. The physician's vehicle followed the prisoner, and behind it came the news media and a coffin draped in black accompanied by the undertaker and his assistants. The gallows were already set up and several thousand people gathered. The prisoner spoke a few words in French contending he didn't understand English well enough to defend himself. He kissed the priest, mounted the scaffold, and within two minutes was declared dead.

The murder of Julia Bulette was avenged, and the crowd returned to Virginia City to open the saloons and celebrate. Throughout the entire event, Julia was never referred to as a woman of easy virtue. It was obvious the people finally accepted the goodness in her, despite her profession.

PROSTITUTION

Prostitution was introduced to America with the arrival of the white man. Until then the Indians had never heard of the custom, no doubt because they had no need for it. As Europeans flocked to America, so did the prostitutes. They came to seek their fortune in the New Land. Eventually, the colonists developed a policy of shipping the unwelcome women back to wherever they came from.

With the westward movement, during the 19th-century, prostitution was tolerated in what was considered a man's country, where there were few women. At the start of the gold-rush, San Francisco had 65,000 men and 2,500 women.

Prostitution, along with drinking and gambling, became a definite part of the rugged West. Although the upright citizens never accepted it...they either endured or ignored it. American's seemed to feel that it was fine for women of other nationalities to participate in prostitution, but not their women. They accepted Indian, black, and Chinese women in the trade...but considered Anglo-Saxon women who were prostitutes, to be immoral.

The so-called "scarlet women" helped to tame the West...miners not only visited them for the pleasures of the flesh, but to have their socks mended and buttons sewn on their shirts. These women provided female companionship at a time when the men were lonely and experienced the daily dangers of working in a mine.

Not all prostitutes were as glamorous or well-paid as Julia Bulette. The grim reality was that most of the women were exploited. Some were poor and illiterate, many were immigrants who spoke little, or no English. These women lived drab lives, often entertaining as many as 50 men in a day, ending up with very little money after paying the madames or pimps.

Few prostitutes ever married. It was common for them to move down the scale of houses as their beauty faded and the years in the profession accelerated the ravages of time. When they became unacceptable to the madames, they were thrown out to become streetwalkers. Suicide, in many cases, was their only means of escape.

There were four levels of prostitution. At the bottom was the streetwalker. She usually worked for a pimp, who in return gave her a measure of protection and affection. The saloon girls were next. They plied their trade in sordid rooms above the bars and dance halls. Then there were the cribs with women of all colors and origins. They took care of the out-of-town transients. At the top were the parlor houses that catered to the exclusive local clientele.

With the influence of "respectable women," tolerance of prostitution was replaced by opposition. In Denver, Colorado, the "ladies" were required to wear a yellow ribbon on their arm as a mark of shame. In retaliation, the madames ordered their women to wear only yellow clothing, from hats to shoes. They presented such an outrageous sight that the law was rescinded.

In its early years, New Orleans was considered the sex capital of America and a mecca for traveling prostitutes. Competition was intense, and the houses became so crowded that prostitutes who could not find lodging, started carrying mattresses on their heads. They were ready to set up business in an alley or open field, whenever the opportunity arrived. Many came west, and the shout "Mattress girl a-comin," would cause a considerable amount of excitement among the male population.

The name "red-light district" is said to have been started in Dodge City, Kansas, one of the most wide-open western towns. The train crews would leave their red lanterns outside when entering a bordello so they could be located in case of an emergency. The madames realized this was an excellent way to advertise and the custom spread.

Today, Nevada is the only state that has legal prostitution...and it is considered one of the tourist attractions. It would appear that, in Nevada, the wages of sin remain very rewarding.

Knowing all of the pitfalls of prostitution, why would a woman in the 1800s enter the profession? Some had no choice. Women were protected by their husbands and families. They bore children, and cared for the home. If her husband died, the woman was without protection, had no income, and job opportunities were rare. She could work for low wages as a domestic, or with a little education, become a schoolteacher. Since working women did not command respect and lived at a poverty level, prostitution became an attractive trade.

In the end, it was all a matter of survival. So, in answer to the question, why would a woman become a prostitute...the answer would seem to be, why not?

Order these exciting books, by Western author Anne Seagraves, today!

DAUGHTERS OF THE WEST, **NEW!** ROUGH, TOUGH, AND IN SKIRTS! Gun-toting ladies capture the feminine side of the west. Stories include "Mustang Jane," who ruled the range with her six shooters, Kittie Wilkens, "The Queen of Diamonds," stagedriver Delia Haskett and the strange saga of "Mountain Charley." —Autographed—176 pages, illustrated $11.95

SOILED DOVES: PROSTITUTION IN THE EARLY WEST A book every woman should read! This stunning book deals with the seamy side of life and tells of the thousands of women who came West seeking fortune and instead found poverty and pain. Caught in a web over which they had no control, most ended up in the world's oldest profession simply because there was nothing else they could do. —Autographed—176 pages, illustrated $11.95

WOMEN WHO CHARMED THE WEST These revealing stories tell of the lives and often shocking love affairs of yesterday's leading ladies. Extoled for their beauty and avoiding disgrace by virtue of their charm, these famous actresses livened up an otherwise drab existence as they entertained the Early West. Lillian Russell and Lillie Langtry were glamorous and indiscreet; Adah Isaacs Menken, a Victorian rebel, and the delightful Annie Oakley won the heart of America. This book contains many portraits from famous collections and articles from her personal scrapbook.—Autographed—176 pages, illustr. $11.95

HIGH-SPIRITED WOMEN OF THE WEST The West is alive! Filled with all the action normally found only in hard-boiled fiction, these true stories bring to life the women who helped shape history. With courage and determination, they left conventional roles behind, becoming America's early feminists. Demanding acceptance on their terms, these high-spirited women proudly took their place in history beside men of the untamed West. Includes stories of Jessie Benton Fremont, Sarah Winnemucca, Belle Star, Abigail Duniway and Helen Wiser, the woman who founded Las Vegas.—Autographed—176 pages, illustrated. $11.95

To order your own autographed book(s), send a check for $11.95 for each separate title, Postage will be paid by the publisher. Residents of Idaho, please add 5% sales tax.

Mail to: Wesanne Publications
P.O. Box 428
Hayden, Idaho 83835